For the "A" Team—
Eugenie Furniss and
Stephanie Cabot

With grateful thanks to the charming Anonymous for his patience, humor, and rather delicious homemade biscuits.

Hotel Babylon

PROLOGUE

All of the following is true. Some of the names have been changed to protect the guilty, but all the anecdotes, the stories, the situations, the highs and lows, the scams, and the drugs, the love, the death, and the insanity are as were described to me by Anonymous—someone who has spent the last fifteen years working at the heart of the luxury hotel industry.

The hotel staff are fictionalized, however, the incidents are real, and the celebrities play themselves, but the stories now all take place in a fictitious hotel known as Hotel Babylon. Narrated by Anonymous, the action is compressed into twenty-four hours. But everything else is as it should be: the rich spend money, the hotel makes money, and the chambermaids still fight the bellboys over a two-pound coin. It's just another twenty-four hours in one of London's most expensive hotels.

Imogen Edwards-Jones,
London 2004

It was a big night last night, and Jesus Christ, do I feel shit. I've got roadworks going off in my head and a tongue like a shag pile carpet. I hadn't really intended to get pissed, but it was Michelle's good-bye party, so I couldn't really help myself. That's the depressing thing about working in the luxury hotel business— you're surrounded by so much hedonism and so much debauchery that, at the end of a long, hard day at the coal-face of the service industry, you just want to get hammered.

We all ended up doing shots at Samantha's on Oxford Street. It's a well-known place, if you work in any of the big hotels in the capital; all you ever need to do is show your hotel ID card and you're in. There were loads of us there last night to see Michelle on her way. Michelle's a popular girl. She's been on Reception with me for a couple of years, and she's leaving this place to go on to Claridge's. Or is it The Dorchester? She's told me that many times, but I can't quite remember.

It was a good night. Plenty of gossip. James, head of Purchasing, who is prone to filling old bottles of 1982 Chateau Rothschild with cheap red wine to impress girls he takes home, disappeared off with one of the waitresses. One of the maids was violently sick everywhere. But the most amazing thing I heard was that one of the girls from Housekeeping caught Michelle giving the manager, Adrian, a blow job. If you knew Adrian, you'd probably be even more shocked. He is one of those posh boys, all stripey shirts, cuff links, and citrus-smelling aftershave. The sort of bloke that you would never expect to drop his trousers in a women's toilet on Oxford Street.

But then again, I have been working in hotels long enough now to know not to judge people by appearances. I learned long ago that it's always the straights in suits who have cases full of rubber and porn mags. It's always the weird-looking blokes who just drink mineral water and go to bed early. And it's always the married women who want to sleep with the staff. But, no matter what they look like, there is one thing they all have in common. They steal—TV sets, teaspoons, ashtrays, bathrobes; drinks from the ludicrously named "Honor" Bar, KitKat candy, crisps; carpets, furniture, works of art. You get men who are shelling out £3,500, or the equivalent of more than $6,000 a night, (not including breakfast) who will piss in a miniature bottle, if it means saving them from coughing up for a Teacher's whiskey from the minibar.

What is particularly problematic about Michelle's behavior last night is that she's got to do her exit interview with Adrian later on today. The exit interview is normally one of those little sit-down chats, where the manager, or the Personnel manager, goes through your strong and your weak points, telling you where you can improve, where you were good and where your particular talents lie. I'd hate to be Michelle. But to be a fly on the wall in that meeting! I hate to say it, but at least that is something to look forward to today.

It's a bit quiet in Reception this morning. My mate, Ben, who is doing nights this week, is nowhere to be seen. I'm a couple of minutes late: It's 7:05 A.M. by the time I have hung up my coat in the staff cloakroom and walked back up the stairs. But Ben shouldn't have clocked off already: he is supposed to wait until I get here, to debrief me on what's been going on overnight.

"Oi, Derek?" I say to the doorman, who is looking a little the worse for a whole night sitting in his leather padded chair. "Any idea where that lazy git of a receptionist is?"

"What, Ben?" asks Derek.

"Yeah, Ben."

"Have you tried in the back office?" he suggests.

"Of course."

There is a small office behind Reception where Reservations makes up the bills, gets faxes, and deals with the ever-changing, ever-annoying occupancy plan on the computer. It is a claustrophobic place that you try and spend as little time as possible in during the day, as it smells of instant coffee, stale cookies, and bad breath. At night, however, its long, flat desk doubles as a bed. Ben has been told off for sleeping in the office before: he is the first face that guests see when they come into the hotel. And because this is a medium-sized luxury hotel, where rooms go from anything from £200 to £2,000 a night, the face they are supposed to see should exude luxury and not be some crinkled, slept-in slob with stapler marks on his cheek.

I walk into the back and, sure enough, he is there. Flat on his back, his mouth wide open, catching flies.

"Oi, Ben! You bastard! Wake up!" I shout.

"What? Shit!" he says, leaping to attention like someone's

shocked his backside with a cattle prod. "Sorry! Oh God, it's you," he mumbles, running his hands through his lank brown hair, looking relieved that he has not been properly busted. "I only dozed off for about five minutes. I thought I'd catch a few before the red-eye guests start coming in from Heathrow."

"Yeah, right."

"Honestly, man, I haven't been here long," he continues, brushing down his rather shiny suit. "What was Michelle's thing like?"

I tell him about Michelle and Adrian and he starts to laugh. He thinks it's the funniest thing he's heard all week. "D'you think he'll talk her through her technique?" He laughs. "Give her marks out of ten?" He says it's almost worth staying up to see her come in at 11:00 A.M. for her exit meeting, and asks me to phone him later with all the details.

He tells me he had a quiet night. Nothing too heavy that he couldn't handle, only a couple of drunks left in the bar that were a bit difficult to shift, and some girl who walked through at 3:00 A.M., swinging a plastic carrier bag full of vomit like it was the latest fashion accessory.

I'll have to ask Derek myself where he thinks the hookers might be when it comes to checking out, or chucking out, later. Ben says he wasn't really paying attention; but we both know that he was either in the bar serving himself a few vodka shots to keep him going, or he was flat on his back in the office.

"Anything else I need to know?" I ask Ben, as I fiddle with the complimentary mints on the counter and click my free hotel pen.

"Not really," says Ben. "Except I gather there is some Yank coming in today. A Texan," he grins. "Chink, chink, chink."

"Everyone loves a Texan," I say to him, giving him a small shove on his way. "I'll see you tonight."

"Yeah, right," he sniffs. "Give me a call when Michelle gets in." He winks. "I'm going to miss her."

"I thought you lost your heart to Jackie."

"Sure, mate," he says, shooting me with his right index finger. "See you later."

Ben's been having this affair with Jackie, the pretty Australian head housekeeper, for at least three months. I've covered for him a few times on Reception, which is how I know. They have the same routine every time: she usually rings down and says something like, "Room 212 needs inspecting." He then runs up the stairs like a dog in heat and they stick a "Do Not Disturb" sign on the door for about half an hour, and then she sends in a maid to clean up the room. It's been going on for a while now, so I thought it might be love, or at least something along those lines. But apparently not.

There is no time to dwell on things, because the phone rings.

"Hello, Reception," I say, as breezily as the seven beers last night will let me.

"Hello," comes this American voice. "This is Room 514."

"Good morning, sir."

"I ordered a breakfast steak about half an hour ago and it still has not arrived," he complains.

"I'm terribly sorry, sir. Have you spoken to Room Service?"

"Room Service, shmoom service," he says. "I keep calling, no one picks up and then I get transferred to you."

"Right, sir, that happens after three or four rings."

"Well, I'd like you to get down there and sort it out for me."

"I can't really do that, sir."

"Can't, or won't?" he asks, beginning to raise his voice. "I have a very important meeting in an hour. If I don't have my steak before I go to the meeting, I'll blame you and the hotel, and I'll invoice you for all the inconvenience you've caused me."

"Right, sir," I say.

"Don't 'right sir' me," he says, becoming really quite irritated. "Do something about it!"

"I'll do it right away, sir."

"Good!" he shouts, and hangs up the phone.

"Room Service?" asks Derek from his leather chair.

"Yep, an American who ordered steak."

"Not again," says Derek. "Why do they do that? What's wrong with a bit of bacon and egg in the morning? Do you want me to go?" he offers.

"Don't worry, mate," I say, thinking I might get myself a swift cup of coffee while I'm down in the kitchen. "I'll go."

"I'll hold the fort, then. Till you get back."

Derek's a decent sort of a bloke. He's been a doorman and night porter for over twenty years and he's worked here for the last five, having inherited this job from his uncle. This place is a bit more upmarket than the four-star heap he used to work, just around the corner. He always says that he'll pass this post on to one of his three sons. He can earn over a grand a week in tips, so it is the sort of job that people like to keep in the family. But the days of passing concierge and doorman jobs on from father to son are almost gone. The trendy modern hotels like The Sanderson and The Metropolitan want male model material posing around outside, while the other establishment places tend to be owned by big corporate chains for whom tradition doesn't actually cut much ice anymore.

"Do you want me to pick you up a coffee?" I ask, as I turn to go downstairs.

"No, don't worry, mate," he sniffs. "I'm off in less than an hour. Then I won't be able to sleep."

Sleep, I think, as I walk down the stairs towards the kitchens and the staff canteen, that's what we all bloody need. No one sleeps properly in this business. It's not even 7:20 A.M. now, and most of the blokes in the kitchen have been up and working for at least a couple of hours. The breakfast chef came in about 5:00 A.M., and he's been parcooking sausages ever since. Not only has he been making up the staff breakfasts since about 5:30 A.M., he's been feeding the guests since 7:00 A.M.

I don't know how the kitchen staff breathe down here: the basement stinks of bleach and bacon, and the air is hot and thick and fogged with the fat of a hundred frying eggs. There's one bloke standing in front of a huge piece of hot, flat stainless steel, flipping; his face is gray and shines with grease, his eyes are glazed and he stares at the eggs in front of him. He looks young, in his early twenties. I don't recognize him at all, but the turnover is quite high down here among the young guys. Who wants to work a fifteen-hour split shift in this hell? But, by the time you've worked your way up through the ranks to a *sous*-chef position, it seems like no one wants to leave. The good chefs get over a hundred thousand a year. If you develop a franchise as a celebrity chef and put your name over the door, you can triple or quadruple that. The bloke doesn't hear me when I shout—perhaps it's the noise of the cooking, or he is just so dog tired, his brain's switched off.

"Oi!" I shout again. This time he moves. "The Yank in 514 wants to know what has happened to his steak?" The chef doesn't say anything, his face barely reacts. Instead, he points with a couple of swift jabbing movements of his pallet knife at a hunk of meat sizzling at the back of the hot steel plate. "How long?" I ask, and he flicks me the V, which I presume to mean two minutes. "Thanks." I nod. "Hurry it up." He doesn't react, and I watch as he just turns to the stack of trays laid up behind him with cutlery, napkins, salt, pepper, and toast and starts sliding the fried eggs onto the plates. Occasionally substituting for the fried a spoonful of scrambled eggs that sit in the large vat next to him, he adds a couple of slithers of bacon from under the hot yellow lights to his left. Down here, it all looks pretty disgusting, yet somehow, after it has made its long chilling journey along various corridors in the hotel and has ended up in the someone's bedroom, it doesn't seem so bad. And they don't come cheap, either—you'll pay anything from £12.50 to £25 for a full English breakfast in one of the capital's luxury hotels, one that costs under 50 pence a plate to make.

I walk out of the kitchen, and the phone in the room next door starts to ring.

"Hello, Room Service," answers another young man dressed in white.

I slope off down the corridor towards the staff canteen for a quick coffee. All this food has made me want a cigarette. The staff canteen is always cold, damp, and smells of cheap cigarettes no matter what food they have on offer. Although, bizarrely, I have to admit that the food they actually serve is not bad at all—bearing in mind they have about £1.20 per person, per day, to feed us all, and most of the staff eat at least two main meals in the hotel every day. We quite often get the leftovers from any banqueting that has gone on the night before; we have the old salads and some of the leftover pastries from the tea. But we also get some good hot pots and stews, the odd chili con carne, and there's always the curries they make for the Bangladeshi cleaners who hose the place down at night. There are a couple of them now, over in a far corner, at the end of their night shift, bent over their food like someone might steal it. Neither of them are talking.

I get myself a cup of black coffee, light a cigarette, and sit down opposite a bloke in a brown Maintenance coat, who I'm pretty sure is Polish. There are certain things that you can take for granted in a hotel. The first is that all Maintenance guys are Polish; the second is that the night cleaners are mostly from Bangladesh; and the third is that the chambermaids are never English.

At another hotel where I used to work, we had this linen porter who actually *was* English. We all thought it was a little odd, but we went with the flow. He was in his fifties. Anyway, one day he broke down, burst into tears in front of all of us in the canteen, saying he couldn't keep it a secret anymore, he had to confess that he'd been in prison for murdering his wife with an axe. He left the next day, and I have never worked with a fellow Brit linen porter or chambermaid since.

The coffee and the cigarette perform their delicious alchemy and my heart starts racing and my brain feels a little more awake. I check my watch and realize that it is already 7:45 A.M. Where the hell did all the time go? I run up the stairs two at a time and steam into Reception. My other half for the day, Liz, greets me with a steely stare.

"Where the fuck have you been?" she says, trying to look stern.

"Downstairs, sorting out some Room Service order," I say. "Anyway, you were late."

"Five minutes," she insists.

There is no point in arguing with Liz. I've got to work with her all day and it is easier to say nothing, as she one of those people who can hold a grudge and give you the silent treatment all morning if she wants to. In her mid-twenties, with blond hair and a great body, she is one of those dolly girls that middle-aged men really fall for. She always has a tan but never seems to go on holiday, her stiff eyelashes curl back on themselves and her fingernails are made of the strongest nylon. She, Ben, Michelle, and I are on a four-days-on, one-day-off rotation that includes a week of nights. But now Michelle has gone, and we're a receptionist down. We're awaiting a replacement, hopefully arriving tomorrow.

"Any problems?" I ask.

"Only one of the waitresses, Marie, has called in sick," says Liz.

"Marie?" I laugh. "I bet she's sick. She went off with James from Purchasing at Michelle's party. What did she say was wrong?"

"Food poisoning."

"Food poisoning? I didn't know you could get that from gin and tonic."

"Yeah, well." Liz shrugs. "Judging by what Derek told me just now about what went on last night, I'm sure she won't be the only one phoning in sick."

"No." I smile.

The telephone goes.

"Hello, Reception?" says Liz in her sibilant heavy voice. "Mmm. Mmm. Right," she says. "I'm afraid we don't actually have the morning-after pill in our First Aid box, madam," she declares. "But if you hang on a couple of minutes, our concierge, Tony, is arriving at eight o'clock, and he will know the closest place it is available. OK?" she asks. "Um, yes, I'll call you as soon as he arrives," she says before putting down the telephone.

"Glad you got that call," I say. "It makes up for the pregnancy-testing kit I had to get last week."

Tony walks through the revolving doors dead on 8:00 A.M. His coat is plush, his suit is sharp, and his shoes are highly polished. His shirt is a crisp Clorox-white and his black tie is from Prada. His dark hair is smooth and parted down the side, and he is sporting one of those contagious grins that make you want to be his friend. There are many things about Tony, besides his smile, that make you want to be his friend.

For starters, there is almost nothing that is going on in London that Tony doesn't know about. He is a veritable *Time Out* magazine. He knows where to go, where to eat, where to dance. He knows the doorman and bouncer at every club worth going to. He knows which Hollywood celebrity is playing which theater and where they drink. He can get you a table at The Ivy, Nobu, Hakkasan, Sheekey's, Petrus, The Wolseley, or Gordon Ramsay's at a moment's notice. He can get you tickets for sold-out shows.

He can get you deals on expensive cars. He can get you girls, drugs, and rent boys. He can get you a villa in the South of France. He knows about this most beautiful place that a concierge mate of his once rented, at great expense, for Courtney Love. It's heaven on earth apparently, not that Courtney would know— she paid the money but never bothered to turn up. But Tony can get you anything—weekends in the country, bus trips around London. He can jump the line at Madame Tussaud's. He can tell you where to get your watch repaired, your shotgun cleaned, where you can find the finest sari material in town. He knows where to late-night shop. He knows where to get a small gift for your wife. He knows just the new shoes you are looking for. He wears his concierge golden keys motif on his lapel with pride, as well he might, because they are the exclusive keys to open any door in town.

"Alright, Tony," I say as he comes in.

"Alright, mate," he says back. Tony's in a good mood. But then again, Tony's nearly always in a good mood. You'd be pretty happy if you took home a couple of thousand pounds a week in tips and bribes and almost none of it ever saw the taxman. "I hear last night was a good one," he adds.

"Yeah," I reply. "How did you know about that already?"

Tony smiles, says nothing and taps the side of his nose. Meanwhile, Derek is up, stretching, and out of here. Tony's arrival, along with the doorman Steve, mean the end of Derek's shift. And as Tony sits down behind his desk, going through his mail, checking through the Cotswold tour pamphlets that he has a ten percent stake in, Steve is already opening the door to a flustered bloke who looks like he's straight off a plane.

"Good morning, sir," says Steve. "Shall I take your bags?"

"Yes, yes," he says, dropping everything at his feet. He walks through the door that Steve holds open and on towards me.

"Good morning, sir," I say, as Liz picks up another ringing telephone.

"Andrew Oliver," says Mr. Oliver, in one of those rootless transatlantic accents that means he could come from almost anywhere. "I have an early check-in," he says. "My secretary organized it," he continues. "Paid the extra in advance."

"Right you are, sir," I say. "I'll just go and check."

There is nothing a hotel likes more than an early check-in or a preregistered guest. It's one of those halcyon-day moments, when the room is double booked. It is a simple process. You get one bloke who pays for his night in the hotel and then, in the meantime, you accept another "early booking" (making this customer pay for the night before to ensure early occupancy). In effect, you are charging for the same night twice. All the hotel has to do is to make sure the first bloke is out before the second bloke arrives. Otherwise, the shit hits the fan.

"Right, Mr. Oliver," I say, picking up his Canadian passport. "We have you booked into Room 514."

"Five-fourteen," he repeats, with a long, relieved sigh that smells of airline food.

"Yes, 514." I smile. Reception, we have a problem. Room 514 is not empty. In fact, Room 514 doesn't look like it will be vacated in the next half hour, and then it has to be cleaned and restocked, and all the while, I'm going to have Mr. Oliver breathing coq au vin down my neck. "Right, 514," I say in such a way that he already knows there's trouble.

"What?" he asks. "There can't be a problem. I've already paid. I've got a fax here to prove it," he says, putting his heavy briefcase on its side and clicking it open.

"No, sir," I say quickly. "It has nothing to do with your booking. We have your booking here." I gesture with my free hotel pen. "It's just that we had a bit of a problem last night. The man who was staying in your room yesterday suffered from um . . ."

"Food poisoning," says Liz. "Terrible, terrible food poisoning. Dreadful. He hasn't been able to leave his room for twenty-four hours. Oysters, I think he said."

"Oysters?" asks Mr. Oliver.

"Yes, oysters," repeats Liz, almost beginning to believe her own story. "No one's been able to move him at all. Doctor's orders."

"Anyway, sir," I say, smiling, "the hotel is full. So I'm afraid we don't have a room available for you at all at the moment. But if you give us half an hour, I'm sure that we can sort something out for you."

"Half an hour," repeats Mr. Oliver weakly. I almost feel sorry for him.

"Yes, sir," I say. "I tell you what," I add, as if the thought has just occurred to me. "Why don't you have a complimentary breakfast in the dining room, eggs and bacon, coffee, that sort of thing, and we'll come and get you as soon as we have a room available."

Poor Mr. Oliver is clearly too tired to kick up a fuss. All he wants is a warm bed, a cup of coffee and CNN on the telly. But instead, he shuffles off in the direction of the dining room, while I take a quick imprint of his American Express Corporate Gold card.

"Well, that went OK," says Liz, with a flick of her blond hair.

"Yeah." I nod. "Better than Ben at the beginning of the week," I say.

Ben had made the terrible mistake of coming out with a rather bad lie when confronted by an irate American, straight off the red-eye from New York. Instead of coming up with the usual food-poisoning story to explain the lack of prereg rooms, he said that there had been a flood, and Maintenance was cleaning it up. The American didn't believe him, and demanded to see the room. Ben said that it wasn't possible, due to its terrible condition. The man called Ben a liar right to his face. Ben said that if the man really insisted he would take him to the room. The American did insist. And Ben took him to a room at the end of the second corridor where we were fortunately having some building work done. But the American still didn't believe him, and asked to see the manager. It all ended up costing the hotel a whole complimentary stay and a bottle of champagne. Adrian was not impressed.

The phones are beginning to go mad now. After eight o'clock, guests start calling up asking you to make up their bills, and members of staff really start calling in sick. And today is Friday, so I'm expecting it to be quite bad: it's always Mondays, Fridays and weekends that are the sick days. The problem has become so bad now that, if you call in sick these days, you don't get paid. If you can provide some sort of doctor's note, then you will get SSP (Statutory Sick Pay) and if not, then tough. Why should the hotel pay for your hangover? Talking of which, mine is feeling pretty bad at the moment. I'd kill for a glass of water and a painkiller.

The telephone goes again.

"Good morning," I say.

"Hello, it's Jacinta," comes a female voice.

It's one of the maids calling in sick. I know she is lying. She knows that I know she is lying, and yet we all go through the same pathetic charade. At least her excuse is slightly different from the usual "food poisoning," claim that I have to pretend to sympathize with. She claims she has something wrong with her "plumbing." I'm not sure whether she means her drains or her womb, so I say something along the lines of "Bad luck, I hope it improves," before hanging up the phone.

Jacinta's a bit late to be calling up and crying off work, as most of the maids and the housekeeping staff should be here before eight o'clock. This is the busiest time of their day, when they should be cleaning and tidying the rooms as quickly as possible—the quicker the turnaround, the quicker they can get through their quota of rooms and go home. Also, the last thing any good hotel needs is a dirty room sitting idle and costing cash. A clean room is supposed to be left just so: two bath towels on the rail (tucked in sideways), washcloths rolled and placed by the basin, towel rail on low heat, white glasses behind the taps; the bathroom door is slightly ajar, the desk lamp is on, the radio is off and the air-conditioning is set at 24 degrees Celsius in the winter and 22 degrees in the summer.

Any chambermaid worth her salt also wants to get into the rooms as early as possible—almost as soon as the guest is thinking about leaving—because some guests leave tips in the room and the last thing they want is either Jez or Dave, the two bellboys, to get in there before them. Last week, I was walking past a room on the third floor and found a twenty-something Portuguese maid and seventeen-year-old Dave fighting over a two-pound coin. Some old hotel hands, who fly and stay all over the world, will leave their tips in bellboy-proof areas such as under the pillows. Others who are less versed in the ways tips can be stolen leave them on the desk in the middle of the room. Then it's up to the maid to run fast to get what she deserves.

And take it from me: the maids really do deserve whatever little extras they get. You wouldn't believe the stuff they come across—dirty underwear, used condoms, sperm-crisp porn mags, lines of cocaine, old syringes, well-used sex toys. People behave so sadly in hotel rooms, the results can be quite shocking. I remember the story of a pop group who had taken so much diarrhea-inducing cocaine, they ended up wiping their arses on the curtains, because they'd run out of toilet paper.

They say that working as a chambermaid has to be one of the

shittiest jobs in the hotel, and when they say shittiest, that's exactly what they mean.

A couple of months ago, this posh middle-aged woman laid an enormous turd in the middle of her bed. It was the weirdest thing. The woman left about nine in the morning, and she had an amusing chat with me as she walked out the door, telling me about the art exhibition she was on her way to see. Meanwhile, she'd left this great big shit in her room and told no one about it. The poor chambermaid nearly passed out when she discovered it. She couldn't work out why the room stank so much while she was cleaning it, until she pulled back the bed sheets and discovered why. The whole thing was so shocking that Jackie in Housekeeping eventually had to clean it up, because the maid simply couldn't face it. What was even more weird was that the woman came back in again in the evening, and made no mention of it at all. She left the next day, and, can you believe this? She didn't leave a tip.

But at least the maids do get tipped sometimes; the chefs downstairs, who work in what I think have to be some of the worst conditions in the hotel, don't even get that. When I say worst, I really do know what I'm talking about, because I had the misfortune to be a chef once. I couldn't hack the bullying, bastard behavior that goes on in the kitchen.

I remember my first day like it was yesterday. If you're not on the breakfast shift you come in around this time. You've got to get your *mise en place* ready, which basically means chopping and preparing all the food prior to service. You're on a split shift, which means that we do eight in the morning to three in the afternoon and then we have from three to five off, which is time usually spent in the pub, or down at the bookies, and then we come back in again until eleven at night. It is so hot and sweaty down there it's like some sort of medieval torture chamber. And the things they do to you: on my first day, they made me stand on a hot stove and explain at the top of my voice why I should be allowed to work in their sodding kitchen. I burnt a hole through the soles of my shoes before they let me get down, and I had blisters on my feet for a week.

As the new boy, I was also made to gut fish and turn potatoes. Turning potatoes is one of those monkey jobs that can send a man mad. It involves topping and tailing a new potato and then taking the skin off the sides in such a way that you end up with a small barrel. When I started out, I could only do about two a minute. By the end, I could work my way through one bucket in about an hour, which roughly works out to about five a minute. I turned potatoes all day, every day, for three months. I ended up doing them in my sleep; I dreamt of those stupid little barrel shapes: it was a nightmare. But at least I got out. There's some South American bloke at The Savoy whose only job is to turn potatoes; he's been doing it for years. I think they managed to get him a chair quite recently, which must have made his year.

There was one thing I did learn about turning potatoes. Although speed is obviously of the essence, it also doesn't do to finish the job too quickly. I did make the mistake once of going up to some *sous*-chef bastard or a *chef de partie* who was on potage, making soups and stuff. I went up to him and said that I'd finished and I had nothing to do. "What? Nothing?" he yelled. "You said you've got nothing to do?" I nodded. "Well, come with me then," he said, and took me into the back of the kitchen where there was a row of three industrial freezers. They're huge things that could freeze a grown man. He opened one of the freezers and, pulling out about six bags of frozen peas the size of pillowcases, ripped every one of them open and poured all the peas back into the freezer. "Right," he said. "I want you to get in there and pick every single one of those peas out of the freezer and put them back in the bags. And don't you ever tell me again that you have nothing to do in the kitchen."

I had to bend over and pick every single one those peas out with my bare hands. It took me three hours, and my fingers were blue with cold by the time I had finished. So, as you can probably tell, I am not overly fond of the kitchens.

I'm not overly fond of Liz at the moment, either. Maybe it's my hangover that's making me a bit more touchy today. Normally, she doesn't annoy me that much. The phone rings again. Liz ignores it, because she is far too busy resting her breasts on the counter, flirting with some fat bloke, asking him how much he enjoyed his stay. So I answer.

"Hello, Reception," I say.

"Hello, this is Room 160," comes this female voice. "I spoke to someone earlier," she says. "About a certain matter."

"Right," I say.

"It is a little sensitive," she says.

"OK. Maybe I can help?"

"Well." She clears her throat. "I rang up to ask if someone could get me the morning-after pill nearly an hour ago and the girl in Reception said that she would get back to me, and um . . . she hasn't."

"Oh," I say. "I'm terribly sorry, madam. If you'll just hold for a moment, I'll see if I can sort something out."

I walk over to Tony, who is sitting at his desk just to the right of the door, counting up how many theater and opera tickets he has sold so far this week, working out just how much his ten percent cut is. He likes this little earner, as he can get up to £400 a month selling *Cats, Les Misérables,* and *The Mousetrap* tickets to guests.

"Er, Tony," I say.

"How can I help you, mate?" he says, looking up from his calculations.

"Morning-after pill?" I ask.

"Oh right," he sniffs. "The chemist at the end of the road," he says. "He does give it to us if we ask, but they do prefer it if the lady goes in herself, as they tend to have to ask all sorts of questions."

"Right," I say. "I get the impression she would prefer it if we went and got it."

"OK then," says Tony, standing up. "I'll send Dave," he says, clicking his fingers at Dave who is standing by the luggage trolley, buffing the brass. Dave, who is twenty-two and eager, drops what he is doing and comes over to Tony. "He could do with exercise. He's been sitting on his backside all morning, haven't you, Dave?"

"Yes, Mr. Williams," says Dave.

"Do you know the room number?" asks Tony.

"160," I say.

"160," he says, his face breaking into a smile. "Isn't that the woman who walked through here last night swinging a plastic bag of vomit?"

"Oh, I don't know," I say.

"I think it is," he says. "I bet she's feeling pretty rough this morning."

"Yeah," I nod. "That makes two of us."

"Yeah, right. Bring on the eleven o'clock exit meeting," says Tony, rubbing his hands together. "I can't wait to see the look on Michelle's face."

Dave walks through the revolving doors on his way out into the sunshine, just as Adrian, the manager, spins in around the other side.

"Morning, sir," says Tony, stacking together a pile of open-top bus tour pamphlets.

"Where's he off to?" asks Adrian, indicating over his shoulder with his left thumb.

"Morning-after pill, sir, for Room 160," grins Tony. "Apparently, it has been one of those nights."

"Really?" smiles Adrian, missing none of Tony's tricks. "I wouldn't know, myself, I've only just arrived. All right?" he says to me.

"All right, sir," I confirm right back.

"Hangover?" he asks.

"No, not at all," I lie.

"Good," he says. "That's what I like to hear. Some professionalism in Reception. Good morning, Liz," he continues, as he walks towards his office.

"Morning, Mr. Thompson," she replies, nodding and giving him her brightest, breeziest service-industry smile.

Adrian is a good-looking man. Tall, with brown hair and green eyes, he has risen fast up the ranks of the hotel corporate ladder, which is unusual for a posh bloke who has got a bit of a player's reputation—for instance, being fellated by a member of the staff is not something that a man in his position is supposed to be doing. He is running a business that has a turnover of some thirty-five million pounds a year. Like the captain of a ship, he should be leading from the front, commanding from a position of wisdom and respect. But Adrian's probably a bit too popular for his own good. The staff like him; he goes to their good-bye parties and misbehaves. He also always organizes a good Christmas event, where he has been known to try and drink the chefs under the table.

He and Tony are good friends, mainly because Tony gets Adrian things—tables in restaurants, tickets to concerts, little deals here, tips there; last year he sent a limo to collect him from the airport when he came back from holiday. He organized Adrian's brother's stag party, making sure they got into everywhere desirable around town and organized a few discounts on the way. And Tony often helps Adrian out of tight spots. In return, Tony more or less gets a free rein to do what he wants. He gets to keep his theater ticket commissions, he gets to organize that we only use one minicab firm, he also gets to plug his trips to Dorset and the Cotswolds, and his Stratford-upon-Avon cheap day trips.

Not that Adrian is the cleanest of cleans. I heard that he was once fired from one of those groovy boutique hotels in France, in one of those upmarket ski resorts. The story is that, when he was a trainee doing nights on Reception, he used to invite all his mates into the hotel after hours and open up the bar, serving free drinks until dawn. Unfortunately, one night when Adrian got particularly plastered, he decided to lie down behind one of the sofas and have a nap. In smaller hotels, anyone doing nights on Reception doesn't usually have anyone else working with him. (Unlike here, where there is always someone else, like the night porter, on duty.) Apparently while Adrian was fast asleep behind the sofa, two thieves walked into Reception and helped themselves to the passkeys and began systematically robbing the rooms. Adrian was woken up to sounds of guests shouting, "*Voleur!* Thief!" as they ran down the stairs, after their belongings.

Adrian's reaction was to leave the hotel before the manager arrived and spend the day skiing, returning the next evening to pick up his paycheck and belongings. The French didn't bother to put it on his record, because he was young and a student and had been working there for free. That sort of economy with the truth happens a lot in hotels.

There was a restaurant manager who worked here for a while, before being fired for stealing. It was only when Adrian actually bothered to ring up the place where he'd last worked that he found out that he'd been fired for the same thing before. But in the last hotel they had come to some sort of arrangement. He had been a good restaurant manager: he had kept the place running smoothly, brought in some celebrity clients and he made such a fuss over everyone who came in that he made it a sort of a destination that the glamorous wanted to be seen at. So they decided to overlook the three cases of wine that he stole, and the way he'd pocketed over £500 in pooled tips, and they cut a deal with him. They promised they'd say that he left of his own accord, and they wouldn't mention his light-fingered indiscretion on his employment record. So he moved over here and he was fine for the first six months or so, bringing in the customers, the paying public, running the place smoothly, then people started to notice things in the monthly audit. It was only a matter of time before he was caught.

We've got a stock check going on later today, or so I have been told. There's a Bombay Sapphire thief in our midst and they want to find out if anything else has gone. Someone has trousered something like seven small bottles of Bombay Sapphire in the last twenty-four hours alone. It's an odd drink to be stealing. It's normally the vodka that goes missing, as you can't smell it on your breath. Either way, it has been going on for a couple of weeks now and it is really beginning to piss Adrian off. He has half a mind to start going through all the chambermaids' handbags when they leave at six o'clock. And that lazy bastard, Mustafa, who sits downstairs in his security booth all day watching day-time TV, never seems to catch anyone.

The telephone rings, and Liz picks it up. It's the guy in Room 302 who wants to check out. I remember him from the day before yesterday. He is one of those sleazy guys with dandruff on his collar and egg on his tie; to be honest, he just looks like he needs a good wash. But Liz has to go to the "little girl's room," and she wants me to take over the call. So I type his room number into the computer in the small office behind the desk, and press Print. Where's that monosyllabic Reservations assistant, Ewan, when you need him? The machine goes crazy, churning out reams of paper with different (976) phone numbers on them. Normally, these phone calls would cost something like 50p a minute, but in the hotel it is £10 for sixty seconds and Room 302 has been hitting the porn lines late into the night. I tear off the sheet and stare. He has been dialing various porn numbers solidly between 2:13 A.M. and 4:02 A.M., and he now owes the hotel the grand total of £850.

It does sound expensive, but he is by no means the worst. A couple of weeks ago, there was this bloke on his own who ran up a £3,000 phone bill over the two days in his room. It was extraordinary. We did call up (when we could get through) a couple of times, and told him that he was running up rather a large bill, but he didn't seem to care. His sister had paid for his room in advance and we did have her credit card swipe behind the desk, so we weren't too nervous. But when he came to check out, he said he could not pay the bill. After much wrangling, we called his sister, who turned up, and hit the roof. Bizarrely, her anger was directed at us for letting it get so out of control. When I finally informed her that we had spoken to her brother on at least two occasions, she became suitably contrite and paid up, or at least I think she has. Adrian came down out of his office to sort it out and I heard the woman make mention of sending a check.

Although Room 302 is not the largest porn chat-line bill that I have seen, I know that it is going to be large enough to cause problems, especially as the man was booked in by his office, and he is clearly on some business trip. It is quite hard to explain an £850 porn bill to one's boss.

I walk back out into Reception with my yard-long bill.

"Oh, dear," says Liz, back from the bathroom. "Don't tell me we've got a talker."

"He looks like he's been a bit chatty," I nod. "That's for sure."

"Porn?" she asks.

"What else?" I ask, beginning to fold up the printout.

"Oh, OK, I don't know," she replies huffily, with an annoying little shake of her offended shoulders. "He could have been on the phone to his wife."

"Yeah, right. No one talks to their wife that much. Anyway," I say, looking up at the sound of the opening elevator. "Keep quiet. Here he comes."

Dandruff-Man approaches the front desk, looking as if he hardly slept a minute last night, which, from his long porn phone bill, has to be the case.

"Good morning, sir," I say. "I trust you had a pleasant stay."

"Very good," says the man, his suit shining in the morning sun. "Slept like a log."

"Good, sir." I smile, handing over the bill half in and half out of the envelope. "Would you like to check your bill, sir?"

"Yeah," he sniffs, as the long length of paper unfurls in front of him. "850 quid!" he says suddenly. "850 quid. You say I've spent 850 quid on the phone?"

"Yes, sir."

"That's outrageous," he says. "850 quid on the phone! You can't charge that."

"I'm afraid that is our standard rate for a premium-rate telephone line, sir."

"Premium-rate! Those aren't premium-rate!" he says.

"I'm afraid they are, sir."

"No they're not!" he says.

"I am afraid they are, sir."

"Will you stop being afraid!" he hisses, his cheeks bright scarlet with anger.

"Please don't raise your voice, sir," I say.

"I did not raise my voice!" he says, raising his voice.

"Fine, sir. Your room is £250 a night for two nights, you have spent £32 in the minibar—"

"On two whiskeys," he says, slapping the top of Reception with his hand.

"Two whiskeys, some chocolate, a bag of crisps and some mineral water."

"Oh, Jesus Christ, crisps and some mineral water," he adds sarcastically. "That really is going to break the bloody bank."

"And you have spent £850 on the telephone."

"This place is daylight robbery," he says, shaking his head, releasing some flakes onto the counter. "I'm sorry, I'm not paying 850 quid on a phone bill," he says. "You should have warned me it would be this expensive, and anyway, they aren't premium-rate lines."

"Hot Honeys is a premium-rate line," I try to explain. "It tells you that as soon as you dial up."

"How do you know?"

"Because we have had many customers use it before."

"Can we come to some sort of arrangement?" he asks.

"I am very happy to make up separate receipts, if you want, sir?" I suggest.

"Right," he says.

"We could also waive about £50 of the bill," I add. I have done this plenty of times before. It usually makes them so grateful that they pay up the rest immediately. It saves an awful lot of fighting, for the cost of £50.

"Really?" he asks, sounding surprised and pleased at the same time. "That would be ever so nice of you."

"No problem, sir."

"Can I put the room on the credit card?" he says, licking his thumb. "And I'll pay the phone bill in cash." He brings up a wad of £50 notes and starts peeling them off, one by one, placing them on the counter. "There we go." He smiles. "800 quid."

"Thank you very much, sir. I'll just run your card through. Would you like any help with your bags?"

"Oh no, thanks," he says, looking down at his small black carry-on. "I think I can manage this."

I walk into the back office with his Green Corporate American Express card and swipe it through the machine. While I stand waiting for the connection, I ignore the miraculously returned Ewan, who is making up a bill for Liz, and stare through the window at the meat van as it pulls up outside the back kitchen entrance below. A man in a white coat and white paper hat starts unloading legs of lamb and sides of beef and pork.

I remember when I was working in the kitchen, the hour

between nine and ten in the morning was when all the deliveries arrived. And God, did you have to be careful, because the scams are endless. And no one's quite sure who is scamming whom, because the products used in the luxury hotel business are so goddamned expensive. The suppliers do the hotel, the staff do the hotel, and the hotel tries to do everyone.

One of the most lucrative scams I heard of went on at The Lanesborough, when the bloke who was in charge of deliveries had something going with the meat supplier. He would order five pounds of Parma ham, for example, when Chef had only ordered two pounds. The hotel would pay for the ten, the delivery man would only take two and the other eight were sent back to the meat supplier, who then sold them elsewhere, splitting the profit with the delivery man at The Lanesborough. The scam ran for about six months, until they were discovered, and the man in charge of deliveries, as far as I can remember, ended up doing time.

But they're all at it. Chef gets bribes from suppliers all the time. Otherwise, why would he choose one Jersey Royal potato supplier over another? They're all clamoring to get their produce into our kitchens—just think of the amount of potatoes we turn a year. At Christmas, you should see the things that come through the back door just to keep Chef sweet. Turkeys, sides of beef, whole salmons, trays of Dover sole, bags of prawns, slabs of foie gras, baskets of truffles; I bet Chef never sets foot in the shops between Christmas and New Year's Day. He sits there, fat as goose, feasting on all his free festive fare.

The suppliers do get their own back, sometimes. They can be quite crafty when it comes to bookkeeping. It is the big orders that you have to be careful of, especially the vegetables. When you have an order as long as your arm, with endives, beans, broccoli, raspberries, blueberries, and cauliflowers, who is going to notice the tray of apples that never arrived? And once you've signed for an order, you can't complain. They're always hassling you into making a mistake. The van always arrives late; you have Chef screaming for his carrots; you have the supplier screaming that he's late and needs to get on with his deliveries; and in the meantime, you have to count through every box of oranges that is on the list, because, if you make a mistake, you're the one who ends up having to pay for it—either with verbal abuse from Chef, or the cost gets docked from your wages.

At the end of the day, Chef likes to balance his books. He is usually on some sort of bonus scheme; I suppose it's a way the management can keep the kitchen under control. If Chef can bring his kitchen within, or even under, budget, then he gets an extra thousand pounds a month or two to three percent of his bottom line. So it's worth his while giving you an earful, not that he is the sort of man that really needs an excuse.

You have to check the quality of the goods over thoroughly as well. It's best to go through them all with a fine comb, as they're always trying to palm off dodgy stuff on you—rotten strawberries, bad cabbages, dead lobsters, soles that are past their sell-by date. Top hotels require top ingredients, in perfect shape. If you're charging up to £45 a main course, it's all got to be good. And usually it is. All the meat served here has had a better life than most of the staff who work this place. Chef appears to know who its parents were, where it lived, what it ate, how much opportunity for play it had, and whether it had a good bunch of mates! I swear he gives more of a shit about the sides of beef that come in here than about the Bangladeshis who clean his floor.

The Green Corporate American Express card is finally accepted, I tear off the slip and walk back out into Reception. Liz is checking out an affluent-looking couple who appear slightly the worse for wear.

"Have you had anything from the minibar?" she asks, her nails clicking again.

"One," replies the young man.

"One what?" asks Liz.

"One minibar," he smiles.

"What one minibar?" asks Liz again, looking confused.

"Yes," says the young man. "One whole minibar, right down to the Malibu."

"Ooh, please don't mention the word 'Malibu,'" says the woman, holding her head. "I can do without being reminded of that."

As Liz tries to work out exactly the cost of a whole mini, I hand over the credit card slip.

"There you are, sir."

"Cheers," he sniffs, depositing some more dandruff flakes on Reception.

"I do hope to see you again soon," I say, as he bends down to pick up his bag.

"Yeah, right," he says, as he walks across the marble floor. "I don't think so."

Liz receives the manager's telephone call asking us to come into the morning meeting. One of us is required to attend, while the other keeps an eye on the front desk. There are always plenty of checkouts to do and someone has to keep an eye out to see if there are any prostitutes left in any of the bedrooms.

Prostitutes are the bane of our lives in the luxury hotel business. Our place is a veritable Mecca for them—a place packed with rich clients whom they are only too keen to relieve of all their cash. And we also have a place that is packed with rich clients who are only too willing to be fleeced. Louche, well-oiled and on their own, buoyed up by business expense accounts, there is nothing they like more than a "quick one" while their wife, or girlfriend, is on the other side of the world. The statistics are amazing: something like seven, out of ten men who stay on their own in a hotel end up asking for "company." We, on the other hand, as a reputable establishment, can't be seen to be condoning prostitution, or even promoting it in any way. But to say that it doesn't go on, to pretend that hoards of whores don't swing through our doors on a nightly basis, and to say that Tony doesn't sometimes have a hand in it or get a bribe out of it, would be a lie of epic proportions.

In fact, the place is overrun with them, and by morning we really have to keep an eye out. Tony knows a fair few of them and if he's done his job correctly, he'll know more or less which guest came in accompanied and which guest ordered up "room service" in the middle of the night. And it is now up to us to make sure that the girls leave. Otherwise, once the bloke has gone off to his meeting in the financial district or wherever he is supposed to be, they start thinking that they're in bloody *Pretty Woman* and start ordering up things like room service, or hairdressing, or a whole load of shit from the concierge service. It is a nightmare, and then, of course, the guest later complains that he didn't order a smoked salmon breakfast at ten-thirty in the morning.

Liz and I have a quick conversation, trying to work out who is going to man the desk and look out for prostitutes, and who is going to the manager's meeting. I have to admit I'm slightly desperate to go the meeting. The idea of sitting down to a milky coffee and a couple of stale institutional cookies on a plate has real appeal to me. So I pull rank.

"I have a feeling we have a couple of important guests arriving today and as the oldest face on the front desk, I do feel I should go," I say, crunching on the pen in my mouth.

"Fine," she says, looking a little annoyed.

"So you'll keep an eye on anything that looks a bit suspicious in the rooms, then?"

"Yes," she exhales, like it is the most boring question she's ever heard.

"OK then." I smile. "See you in a while."

"Have fun," she says sarcastically.

I walk towards the glass double-swing doors that lead into the main lounge area. It is 10:10 A.M. and already there are a couple of skinny women with stiff blond hair, wearing gold and beige, who are smoking, drinking coffee, and have a meeting of some sort. The lounge area is an odd mixture of old and new. The walls are covered in mirrors with fabulous old gold lamps that give the place a decadent French air, yet the furnishings are quite modern: fat sofa, leather chair, low gold-leaf tables. It is an odd mixture, yet it works well enough for us to have a constant troop of fashion models coming to have their photos taken here. Past the corridor that leads to the bar, and in the far corner of the lounge area next to an enormous golden statue holding a flaming torch lamp, is the door to the manager's office.

Actually, he has a suite of offices. He has a sort of outer office, where his secretary, Angie, works, and where all the important faxes for the hotel are delivered. To the left he has this inner office, which is all wooden panels and leather, with an enormous desk along one side of the room, where he sits backlit by the window. Just off to the right of Angie's desk is another much larger office with a conference table in the middle, surrounded by high-backed chairs. The wood-paneled, leather-padded office is used when he is charming a bride to shell out £25,000 on her wedding, and for when he wants to shout at staff. The large conference room is used every day for the morning meeting, which is attended by almost everyone.

They include Jackie, the blond-haired head of Housekeeping (who is having an affair with Ben), representing the cleaners and chambermaids, and James, the sandy-haired head of Purchasing, as well as the food and beverages manager, the banqueting and events manager, the Maintenance manager, the head of Security, normally the Personnel manager, but today he is off on honeymoon, and the Restaurant manager and the head chef, who do all the talking when it comes to the food. Tony turns up, as does Gino, the head barman, Lynette, the manager in Reservations, and I or someone else from Reception, to keep Adrian up to date.

Every morning the meeting starts the same way. Angie, who exudes all the faded grandeur of one of the golden statues in the lounge, comes in with her hard, pale yellow hair, pink lips and lavender-scented cardigan. She is carrying a tray that sports a large silver pot of coffee and another, similar, pot of tea, a jug of milk, a pot of sugar, and a plate of assorted cookies. There is usually some sort of initial holding back on the cookie front, when everyone carefully picks a dry Rich Tea or some other bland brand, and it is only on the plate's second journey around the table that anyone attempts to go for a Bourbon cookie. But we are always careful that there are two chocolate digestives left for when Adrian comes in late, which he always does, every morning, hot off the telephone from someone important.

"Morning, morning, morning," he says, walking brusquely to the head of the table, smoothing down his pink- and blue-striped silk tie as he goes. Adrian loves ties; he has a large collection, mostly given to him by guests. The guys from the Gulf states, who pack the place during August and drop tens of thousands in a month, tend to give him three or four Hermès ties at a time. But today's jaunty number is looking a bit on the cheap side. Perhaps Dave forgot to collect all the others from the dry cleaners? "Right," he says, sitting down. "Anything in the duty manager's logbook that I need to be aware of? Any horrors? Any nightmares?"

The manager's meetings are normally quite serious affairs. In the smaller hotels they can be quite amusing. In the small hotel I worked in previously, we all used it as an opportunity to chat and have a laugh, and a bit of a bonding session. Someone would have certainly mentioned to Adrian something about last night's little indiscretion and we might have had a joke at his expense.

But when the hotel is as big as this one and there is thirty-five million pounds' worth of customer business to deal with, plus all the glitches and the problems that occur, we only ever have such joking when Adrian is in the mood. And today it seems he is quite talkative. Perhaps he is trying to pretend that he is part of the group because of what he did last night; he is, forgive the pun, sucking up to us a bit.

I tell him about the woman walking through the lobby with the bag of vomit, and he laughs. I also tell about the man who shouted and screamed about his porn bill, and I mention the little problem about the preregistered Canadian whom we failed to room as he came off the red-eye. Adrian congratulates me on my fifty-pound discount, saying it sounded like the best way of calming the man down, and he notes the new room number of the overtired Canadian and declares that we should send up a bottle of champagne. He takes a look at the duty manager's (Gavin's) book, and asks Chef to explain the problem that the American businessman had with his early morning steak. Chef's at a loss, and blames it on someone junior and promises to give them the dressing-down of their lives.

"That's all very well," says Adrian. "But because you didn't do your job properly, getting the steak out in time, the Canadian couldn't check in at all. We are all mutually dependent," he says. "We are a team, and we must function as a team." Chef mutters something into his whites. "I know it's difficult, Chef," placates Adrian. "But that's why you get paid three times more than anyone else in your kitchen. Anyway," he continues, "Lynette, what have you got for us?"

Tall, thin, and mousy, with double-glazed vision like a wombat, Lynette takes her Reservations position very seriously indeed. It's her job to go through the list of VIP guests arriving today and decide who gets a half or a full bottle of complimentary champagne, who gets a wallet with the hotel's name in it, who gets a teddy bear, a candle, or some other "loyalty treat." Ten stays gets a champagne, and five stays, a teddy bear or something like that. She stacks her pages on the table and for some reason feels that she should stand up. This clearly amuses Adrian, because he breaks into a smile.

"Well," says Lynette. "We have a few things. Firstly, the difficult Mrs. Dickson is back."

"Right," says Adrian. "I thought we were going to have her blacklisted."

"Yes, well," says Lynette. "It is quite difficult to do that, seeing as her husband has shares in the company. No amount of telling her that we are full is going to put her off. She feels she owns the place and, by rights, I suppose at least her husband does, a bit. Anyway, she is bringing her Yorkshire terrier this time, so someone will have to be around to walk it—"

"It's like having Geri Haliwell to stay," interrupts Adrian, with a large laugh. He is definitely trying to pretend that he is one of us today. We all smile: we've all heard his Geri Haliwell story before. How, while at the Halcyon, where she stayed after her house was burgled, there always had to be someone on hand to walk her wretched little dog, Harry. He says how much everyone hated that goddamn dog. Then he usually goes on to say how she ordered some running machine to be put in her room for around £8,000, and how she only used it to hang her clothes on. She apparently lived on club sandwiches and room service. She never ate in the restaurant, and would send people out for food all the time.

Everyone laughs.

"Yes, well," says Lynette again, after allowing a suitable pause for group amusement. "So I have put her in the only room she hasn't complained about so far."

But Adrian isn't finished. "That reminds me," he says, clicking his fingers. "Do you remember the story about Richard Gere who made the Hyde Park Hotel change its carpets? He said he couldn't bear the spotted stuff they had in all their rooms, so they refurbed one at vast expense, and he never came to stay there again!"

"Yeah!" laughs Tony. "Didn't they also put in an extra large shower for Pavarotti because he couldn't get in the bath?"

Adrian laughs. "Honestly, the things we do."

He then launches into his favorite story about Michael Jackson and his Evian bath: forty-eight bottles of the premium drinking water, poured into his bathtub at The Lanesborough, one after the other, apparently. It hardly came halfway up the sides, and even then, the water was cold. To this day, Adrian has no idea what he did with it. Perhaps he just got in, and then added the hot water from the tap. Adrian shakes his head, "No idea."

"Yes, well," interjects Lynette. "We also have Mr. Masterson arriving today."

"Mr. Masterson?" asks Adrian.

"The Texas oil baron."

Adrian must be feeling dreadful; his brain can't be working at all. Everyone else around the table knows exactly who Mr. Masterson is and we're all sitting up accordingly. A fat, florid, ebullient Texan, he acts like the guy who invented tipping. He never stops handing out ten-pound notes. When he's staying in the hotel, you'd be amazed how few people go off sick.

"He has sent through a request for some Trinidad Diplomatics to be placed in the hotel humidor," says Lynette.

"Some what?" asks James, his posh blond hair flopping over to one side.

"Trinidad Diplomatics. They go for £500 a cigar at The Lanesborough," declares Lynette rather smugly, like a girl who has done her homework, which she clearly has.

"I've never heard of them," says James.

"What!" declares Gino, watching the profits from his bar disappear before his very eyes.

"Keep your hair on, mate," says James, leaning forward. "My cigar dealer is turning up in about half an hour. I'm sure he'll know where to get his hands on a couple of boxes."

"A couple of boxes!" repeats Gino, like someone has been sick on his shoes.

"Look, man," says James. "There's no point in asking Hunters & Frankau at this short notice. I'll have to see."

"I have no desire to know whom you are dealing with," says Adrian, with a wave of his hand. "Just so long as the hotel is properly stocked."

"My caviar bloke is arriving today as well," smiles James.

"Good," says Chef.

"Where's he from this time?" asks Adrian.

"Some trawler in the Caspian, via Iran and then Frankfurt, I think," says James. "Anyway, it's half the price."

"And I hope that the saving will be passed on to the hotel?" asks Adrian.

"Of course," says James, in a manner that implies some of the so-called savings might end up elsewhere. "I have also a rare cognac and brandy sale today."

"Great, of course, it is today," grins Gino, clapping his hands with delight. "You have my list already?"

"Yup," says James, patting his top pocket. "I have already spoken to Sotheby's and we have reserved that 1802 JBE Massougues cognac that your Japanese friends like so much."

"Excellent," says Gino, looking forward to selling that at five hundred pounds a shot.

"And I'm hoping that bastard, Salvatore, at The Lanesborough won't get his hands on the bottles of 1800 Bignon brandy that I've heard are still up for grabs. You know, that one that you like, selling for seven hundred pounds a shot," says James, biting the end off his Bourbon cookie.

James has one of the best jobs in the hotel: not only does he spend all his time flicking through fancy catalogs looking for fine wine sales and whiskey, cognac, and brandy auctions, spending somebody else's money, but he also gets to go on all these amazing trips abroad. He gets invited to stay in the champagne Chateaux in Riems in France, as a guest of Veuve Clicquot or Moët et Chandon and gets pumped full of champagne and foie gras. They drown him in hospitality to thank him for his orders and in the hope that he will order more. He gets to go and see the juniper harvest in Tuscany as a guest of the gin company. And then someone will fly him to the South of France to look at some new soft cheese. Much like Chef at Christmas, when James comes in to work, it is essential that he bring his car. He gets so many free gifts, hampers, cases of wine, sides of salmon, there is no way he could get all his bribes home on public transportation.

He and Chef also have plenty of deals going on between them. For example, James might suggest a new brand of olive oil, and when Chef orders thirty-five bottles of the stuff, both he and Chef get a couple of quarts free. The same goes for more luxury items like smoked salmon or more obscure products like game: the kitchen takes twenty-four pairs of grouse, and Chef and James divide up the ensuing perks between them. I heard that his ex-girlfriend threw up last year on all the free chocolates he was given for Christmas.

"I'm afraid I have to go," announces Chef, getting up from his seat. "I have the cheese man arriving in about ten minutes at the back door. If you have any Celine Dion requests like tara-masalata and pita bread in every room, just give me a call."

All I can think of is the cheese man, as Chef runs out of the door. My stomach is rumbling despite the three cookies I have just eaten. The cheese man used to be one of my favorite things when I worked in the kitchen. He turns up every other day in his small van and parks outside the back of the hotel. Then Chef, or sometimes one of the *sous*-chefs, goes out and sits in the van to taste slithers of delicious cheese from all over the world. He chooses anything from whole Stiltons and strong cheddars for the cheese board, to feta for the salads. The choice is vast and the smell, once you get inside the van, is overpowering. Sometimes you get little squares placed on crackers to taste, sometimes he hands over slices that are almost transparently thin and melt on your tongue, building their flavor up the back of your nose. What I wouldn't give to spend twenty minutes in the cheese van to gorge myself on treats.

And he's not the only one who is queuing up for Chef's approval right now: The man who sells mushrooms is there, with his basket of morels and carefully wrapped truffles; perhaps even the fish dealer with his trays of hake; and there used to be a man who brought in sea urchins from France. They'd come on the early flight into Heathrow, clear customs, and they'd make it to the hotel by about now. But I don't know if there is much call for that sort of thing anymore: sea urchins were very late eighties, don't you think?

Lynette continues to run through her list of guests, reiterating that we have to be extra nice to Mr. Masterson and the shareholder's wife with the dog. She also announces that there is some drinks affair on in the Banqueting Hall tonight, and that we should keep an eye out for drunken waifs and strays and anyone who looks like they haven't been invited.

"Right," says Adrian with a clap of his hands. "That all looks about OK. Anyone have anything they want to add? Housekeeping?"

"No, fine," says Jackie. "Only just reminding everyone that there is an outside stock checker coming in today."

"That's correct," says Adrian. "They have been specifically told to do the bar."

"Shit," says Gino, his head slowly falling into his hands.

"Sorry about that, mate," smiles Adrian. "Anyone else?" he asks. "Good," he says. "I'd better get on, I've an exit meeting to perform. I'll see you all later."

"Right," I say, gathering up my pieces of paper as quickly as I can. I don't want to hang around for a chat. I'm going to have to leg it back to Reception if I'm not going to miss Michelle's imminent arrival.

I arrive in Reception at a jog. Liz has never seen me so keen to get back to my post after the management meeting. Normally I'm loitering around having a cigarette downstairs, sneaking in a quick cup of coffee, before coming back out front. But my face is quite pink by the time I reach the desk. I'm sure I'm sweating out last night's alcohol.

"Has she come through yet?" I gasp.

"Who?" asks Liz, stapling bits of paper together.

"Michelle, of course!" I say.

"Oh, her," sneers Liz. These two have never been the best of mates. Cut from the same cloth, it is unfortunate for Liz that Michelle's cloth is just that bit younger, perkier, and possibly of higher quality. "She hasn't shown her face yet."

"Oh good," I smile. "I'd hate to miss her."

"I can't say that I am terribly interested."

"Oh," I say, looking around. "Where's Tony gone?"

"He's gone to help Jez and Dave get rid of a woman on the third floor," says Liz.

"Right. I missed that."

"Yeah," smiles Liz. "While you are thinking about Michelle, the rest of us are getting on with our jobs."

She tells me that Jaguar was in last night and that she has had problems trying to get her out of Mr. Mayes's room after he has gone to work. The whole thing comes as a bit of a surprise: Ben didn't even tell us that Mr. Mayes checked in last night. He must have done it quite late. But Mr. Mayes can almost check in whenever he likes. He is a hotel regular: he's way beyond the complimentary wallet stage. He lives in Manchester, and he comes down to stay in the hotel about three times a month. He works in the entertainment industry, and parties like crazy when he stays here. He always orders a couple of bottles of Cristal champagne from Room Service and he always takes a couple of grams of coke. He's not very discreet about it: it is all we can do to stop him from chopping it out in the honor bar. And he always has a hooker with him. He has four favorites that he's named after cars—Mercedes, Jaguar, BMW, and Roller. We all turn a blind eye to his activities because he drops so much cash in the place, but some days, the girls can be difficult. And today sounds like one of those days.

"She's ordered breakfast and I had to tell her she couldn't have any unless she was prepared to pay cash," says Liz. "And then she just shouted at me on the phone. She was F-ing and bitching and she kept on saying that if we didn't let her have breakfast on the house, she and the other girls would take their business elsewhere. She said something like Mr. Mayes spends about five grand a month in this hotel and if we wanted his custom, we would have to accommodate her."

"That sounds messy," I say.

"It was. So, as soon as Tony came out of the meeting, I sent him up to sort it out."

"Good idea," I say. Tony is always getting sent up to sort out the hookers; that's part of his job.

Then, just as we are talking, Tony comes out of the elevator with Jaguar in tow. She is an amazingly attractive woman: long legs, long dark hair, and great breasts, she could be a model if she weren't a prostitute. She swans out of the front door in her high black boots, giving Tony a little friendly wave as she goes.

"Jesus Christ, Tony," I say, as she walks out the door and up the street. "What did you say to Jaguar?"

"Nothing too bad," he grins. "Something along the lines that Mrs. Mayes was due in the hotel any minute, and if she wanted to keep her rather lucrative agreement with Mr. Mayes going, I suggested that she should run for it before the wife showed up."

"Good thinking," I say.

"The old ones are always the best," says Tony. "They work everyti . . ."

His voice peters off into nothing. He stares at the main door where Michelle's getting out of a cab, ten minutes late for her exit interview. She is wearing a pair of knee boots, flesh colored tights and a very short miniskirt. It's a combination not dissimilar from the recently departed Jaguar. She looks a lot more attractive out of her dark suit and light shirt that she usually wears on Reception. Steve's mouth hangs open as she strides through the revolving doors, her head held high. Even Dave stops polishing his brass.

"Morning, everyone," says Michelle, her Australian accent still audible after three years over here.

"Morning, Michelle," says Tony. "Good farewell party?"

"Excellent, thank you," she replies without breaking her stride.

"Looking forward to talking to the head? Or should I just say, giving head?" he laughs.

"Ha, ha, ha," says Michelle sarcastically, heading for the glass swing doors. "At least I'm getting out of this place."

"Oooh," says Tony, pretending to sound impressed. "Onwards and upwards to The Savoy? I hear the manager's very accommodating."

"Piss off," says Michelle, standing between the two doors, giving Tony the finger.

"Enjoy your exit," smiles Tony. "You've given us all great pleasure."

"Yeah, right," says Michelle, rather weakly.

"Some of us more than most," says Tony.

Jez and Dave snort with laughter. Only Liz doesn't seem that interested. She is busying herself by pleasantly directing a couple of Home County women in corduroy skirts and fun sweaters, clutching plastic shopping bags, towards the lounge for their midmorning coffee. Lady day-trippers love this place: we are not far from Sloane Street, and are within an easy cab ride from all those destination shops they seem to enjoy so much, like General Trading and Peter Jones. During sale season, we have at least twenty or thirty women drinking coffee and snacking on home-made shortbread at any one time. Their conversation always seems to be dominated by bargain bed linen and the price of home furnishing materials. But the hotel loves them because they cost us almost nothing. A pot of coffee and some cookies cost us less than ten pence per person, and they're charged ten pounds plus service for coffee for two. Morning coffee women are one of those excellent little earners that really should not be sniffed at. They don't make much mess, they don't hang around very long, and they require minimal maintenance. The hotel couldn't be happier.

The bar staff also seem to be in a good mood as they walk in through the door. They are laughing and talking in Italian. They are nearly always Italian. There are three of them who work in our main bar, Alfredo, Francesco, and the ever-loyal Gianfranco, who follows our head barman, Gino, wherever he goes. They are all friendly, good-looking blokes, but they don't really mix that much with the rest of us. I think it has something to do with the hours they keep. They come in just after 11:00 A.M., and they don't leave until the last man standing in the bar decides it's time to go to bed. Their long hours are more than made up for in tips, and the later they stay, usually the more drunk the customer, and the fatter the tip. There is nothing they like more than a gang of guys from the Gulf states cracking open a few of bottles of 1919 Dalwhinnie whiskey and really going for it, sucking on their Monte Cristo Number Twos. There was a legendary session that I heard about that went on last August, when this group of Saudis dropped eighteen thousand pounds in one evening in the bar. They added a thousand-pound tip that was divided around the bar. We didn't hear the end of it for weeks.

Tony's obviously determined to wipe the smiles off their faces this morning because, when they are halfway across Reception, he shouts.

"Hey, you lot!"

"What?" asks Gianfranco, turning around.

"Looking forward to your stock check today?"

At the mere mention of the words "stock check," all their shoulders slump.

"Don't tell me you've forgotten?" laughs Tony.

"Don't tell me we weren't told," replies Gianfranco.

"Oh, dear," smiles Tony. "Enjoy yourselves, boys."

No sooner do the barmen disappear through the glass doors to change into their black ties and set up in the bar beyond, than the outside auditor arrives. He is wearing a calf-length overcoat and is carrying a briefcase and a clipboard.

"Good morning. I'm Mr. Kent," he says, as he puts his clipboard down on the counter. "I am from Hotel Auditing and I have an appointment with the manager, Mr. Thompson."

"Right, sir," I say, reaching for the telephone, marveling at his imaginatively named company. "I'll just call through, and tell them that you are here."

The announcement of Mr. Kent's arrival is enough to send a frisson of fear throughout the whole hotel. Word gets around very quickly that some outside bod has come to check up on everyone. And there is nothing that hotel employees hate more than a stock check, particularly in the booze department.

The problem with alcohol is that most of us think it is one of the perks of working in a hotel to take a quick sip, or a shot, to help with the working day. Gino and I are always having a few glasses here and few glasses there, to help us get through a difficult night. He often comes through with a small glass of brandy or vodka and slips it on the Reception counter for me. It is totally against company policy but normally everyone turns a blind eye to this sort of behavior. Unfortunately, the whole point of an outside auditor is that they pick up on these things. They sell themselves to hotel managers as the sharpest eyes in the business, and the money paid for an outside audit is supposedly more than made up for by the things that they spot and the cash that is saved.

In the old days, petty pilfering used to be a whole lot easier. You'd slip off with a half-drunk bottle of vodka here, or you'd walk off with a Baileys around Christmas time, to save you buying one on the way home to give your mum. It was always the gins, the vodkas, and the Baileys that went, for some reason. The whiskeys and the wine weren't ever really touched. Mainly because they are all kept in this special cellar that stores the wine at a perfect temperature, the bottles are turned regularly by the cellar man, and you need two sets of keys to get in. Although, if you really did put your mind to it, all things were possible. But nowadays, since we converted to the computer system, it is a whole lot more difficult to help oneself.

There are a few tricks of the trade that still work. The old one of filling up empty vodka and gin bottles with water and placing them behind the bar does work, just so long as no one spots what you are doing. Another trick involves short-serving the customers. When they ask for a double, you serve a single, charge for a double and hope that they don't notice. If they are drunk enough, they usually don't. You then keep track of how many shots you served short, and by the end of the night, you can get up to a couple of bottles of vodka that the whole bar has sort of chipped in for. You can each average more than a free bottle of vodka a month.

The auditor does also pick up on bottles of water and mixers that the bar staff have genuinely forgotten to charge for. And, of course, ullage—the slips and spills, the late-night sloppy pourings that, after a while, get to equal a whole bottle of gin. This is the sort of stuff that we actually have to pay for. The management reserves ten percent of what the guests pay in tips and service charge to pay for breakages, theft, and shortfalls in the till. When a bottle of Hildon Water is forty pence a bottle at cost, sold to customers for upwards of three-and-a-half pounds, then the cost-price shortfall isn't usually that much. However, if you happen to have a Bombay Sapphire thief in the hotel, then this month's ullage and theft bill could be quite large.

As Mr. Kent is dispatched to annoy Gino in his bar, another rather seedy-looking bloke arrives, talking on his cell phone. He has dark curly hair to the shoulders and a suit that shines in certain lights. He is carrying a heavy-looking holdall bag. But before he has a chance to introduce himself, James flounces across the hall, hand out, smooth shake at the ready, and ushers him into his back office.

"Who do you think that was," I ask Liz. "Cigars or caviar?"

"Cigars," says Liz.

"How do you know?" I ask.

"I recognize him from before. He comes every couple of months, with a very heavy bag and leaves with nothing but a smile on his face. Anyway," she adds. "The caviar guys always look Eastern European and smell of salted fish. That bloke looked Latin to me."

"Mm," I say, with a small shrug. "I think I might go for lunch."

Liz agrees. She is on a diet and doesn't really want to go. She shows me her Slim-Fast bar that she has underneath the leather diary and tells me not to be too long.

Downstairs, it is busy in the staff canteen. Devoid of air and natural light, the rows of tables and chairs shine under the neon strip light and the air smells of onions, sweat, and high-tar cigarettes. I pick up a plate and walk along what I suppose could be called the salad bar. There are some sliced tomatoes and basil that look like they were out flaunting themselves at a banquet the night before. There are bowls of rather jaded-looking lettuce and a large bowl of canned sweet corn with some red peppers. I turn up my nose; even the large bowl of pasta and canned tuna looks like it has seen better days. I walk over to the hot section where all the food was put together at some stage yesterday afternoon and reheated today for our delight and delectation. As it is kept under large hot catering lamps, it is advisable to peel off the skin before serving. Two young *sous*-chefs are dolloping out the chili. I get myself two-spoons' worth and pick up a hunk of white bread. Sometimes I do try and eat healthily, but today is just not one of those days.

Looking up and down the rows of seating, I see the chair next to Alfredo, Francesco, and Gianfranco is taken. To tell you the truth, I am slightly relieved. I would only have to listen to them moaning about their stock check all lunchtime, so I decide to go off and sit with the chambermaids and a minibar attendant.

"Hi," I say, as I sit down amongst three of them. They stop talking Spanish or is it Portuguese? (I always knew I should have worked harder at school.) None of them say anything. They are all quite a lot older than me—in their forties or early fifties. Most of them, I should imagine, have children, and those are hoping to do better than their parents. Well, it wouldn't be hard: earning four pounds fifty pence an hour and fighting with bell-boys over tips is not the sort of job most people aspire to. And that's in a reputable place like this, and only if they're legal.

"Good morning?" I ask, by way of trying to make conversation.

"Not really," replies the woman sitting in the middle. "I have had to cleaning two used condoms, and someone left a old tampon in the bath."

"I'm very sorry," I say, shoveling some chili into my mouth. "That doesn't sound very nice."

"I think I have broken a riding crop," says the woman on her left, putting her hand over her mouth.

"What?" I say, looking up.

"I was vacuuming in front of the cupboard, when the door fell open and this stuff came out," she says. "Fluffy handcuff things, this rubber suit, and a whip, which I shut in the door by a mistake, and I think I have broken it. Jackie says I have to wait until she has spoken to the owner, before I know if I have to pay."

"Right," I say, not really knowing how to respond.

"And I discover three KitKats which have been stuffed with cardboard and put back in the minibar," says the minibar attendant.

"I hate it when that happens," says the one in the middle. "The effort that goes into making a whole KitKat," she sighs, her eyes rolling in her head. "You think that it was easier to pay."

"And," says the maid to the right. "They found Anna Maria asleep on one of the beds this morning."

"No!" says the woman in the middle, sitting back in shock.

"Oh yes," nods her friend on her right. "Television on, door closed, the whole thing. Fast asleep on a bed that she had just made."

They all shake their heads disapprovingly. These women all work hard and, for some reason, they seem to take pride in what they are doing. Why they would take pride in putting a chocolate on someone's pillow or placing a facecloth at the correct forty-five-degree angle from the basin, is anyone's guess. But apparently they do. I take a bite of my bread, and thank my lucky stars that I don't have to deal with skid-marked sheets for a living. At least, I have the possibility of moving on and up in my job—to duty manager and possibly to a manager. Working in hotels is all I ever wanted to do from the age of six. I swear it was a childhood dream of mine, to work my way up and maybe have a hotel of my own one day. But these women sitting opposite me can't even dream. It's terrible: they are destined to clean up after other people forever. Chambermaids don't get promoted; they just get fired. Even the head housekeeping job is usually given to some girl on a management traineeship. Chambermaids start cleaning up toothpaste, and they end cleaning up toothpaste. They get their four and a half pounds an hour, their two to three meals a day, and the occasional fiver from some passing American. It makes me depressed just sitting here. I wipe my plate down with my last remaining bit of bread and contemplate going downstairs for a cigarette.

I walk into the staff smoking room and immediately realize the error of my ways. I haven't noticed how late it is. It's 11:55 A.M. and the place is full of all the *sous*-chefs, commis chefs, and kitchen porters having their final cigarette before the lunchtime hell begins. The pale green walls sweat with smoke; I almost can't see across to the other side. I can't sit in here for a quick puff, because every guest who arrives in the hotel will smell smoke on my suit. So I wander slowly back upstairs.

Back on Reception, and Liz is having a few problems with late checkouts. It is always noon when you suddenly discover that a couple of guests haven't vacated their rooms. Sometimes, one of the chambermaids calls up to tell the desk that she can't get into a room because it has a "Do Not Disturb" sign on the door. Or sometimes, you notice on the computer that a couple of rooms that should have turned green on the screen and be VI (vacant and inspected) are in fact still red, or OD (occupied and dirty). Checkout time here is actually 11:30 A.M., and we tend to run quite a tight ship. If someone actually asks to stay on for longer, then we will allow them until 2:00 P.M. before we start charging them. Otherwise, they can expect a telephone call asking them if they want to be charged a half-day rate for continuous occupation of the room, or if indeed they plan to stay another extra day. We aren't being rude—it's just that the maids have so many rooms to get ready before the new guests start arriving, we need that time to turn things around.

"I am sorry to disturb you, sir," Liz is saying when I arrive. "But checkout is 11:30 A.M. and it is now midday. Will you be vacating the room shortly?" I can tell the man is angry because Liz winces slightly as he shouts in her ear.

"I am terribly sorry to hear that, sir," she says. "Perhaps, if you came down to Reception, we could look into the matter." He says something back, and obviously hangs up.

"OK?" I say.

"Fine," she sighs. "He says he's had a hundred pounds stolen from his room and that he is holding us responsible."

"Oh right," I nod. "I bet it is another one of those guys who were so pissed last night they forgot they spent it."

"Probably," says Liz. She turns and smiles at me.

"What?" I ask.

"Will you do me a favor?"

"OK."

"The thing is, there is another room that hasn't checked out, and so far, he is not responding to calls. I have rung the room half a dozen times and there is no reply. Could you just go up and see what is going on?"

"Do you think we have a stiff on our hands?" I ask.

"Don't be silly," dismisses Liz. "It's just a little odd, that's all."

I take the elevator up to the third floor. I am far too tired to take the stairs. When I arrive, the corridor is buzzing with action. There are two Polish maintenance guys right outside the elevator trying to mend a wrinkled carpet. Further along, there's a monosyllabic cleaner who is vacuuming the thing. Looking at it, I would say the carpet really does need replacing; in fact, I think it lets the hotel down: red with a gold strip along the edge, it is bald, shiny, and threadbare in places. What we really need is a rock star band to behave badly and we'd all be happy.

There is nothing like a celebrity behaving appallingly to help finance a makeover. I know of one hotel that had their whole dining room refitted, carpets, wallpaper, and everything, after a band started a food fight. The manager had a conversation with their manager about how much "damage" the band had done, and then sent them a cleaning-up invoice that financed a makeover of epic proportions. It was the hotel that cleaned up in that incident. Then again the hotel always cleans up.

Just in front of the bloke vacuuming, I find the room. There is no "Do Not Disturb" sign on the door, so I knock loudly. There is no reply. So I knock again. I use my plastic passkey, or Ving card, to let myself in. The place is a mess. The chambermaid is waiting for the guest to check out before she can do anything, yet he is nowhere to be seen. I check the bathroom: nothing. The best thing I can do is telephone Lynette in Reservations to see if we need the room back today; otherwise, I am inclined to leave it and wait for the guest to return and then sting him for the extra day. I call Lynette from the room and she starts to have kittens on the telephone. The hotel is overbooked by twenty percent at the time of speaking and she is desperate to get the room back. Lynette always overbooks the hotel if she can, because, since the advent of the cell phone, people are always canceling rooms at the last minute or changing their bookings. Business moves so fast these days that no one can guarantee anyone will be where they say they will be at any one time. So she overbooks, and availability can change as much as thirty times in one day. Lynette is so good at juggling, she should be in the circus. But, at the moment, she is being a pain in the arse. She is kicking up a bit of a stink, telling me that the man must leave his room, he hasn't booked for an extra night and she has a couple from Lancashire on a wedding anniversary weekend that are arriving this afternoon.

I stand and think for a bit: what am I supposed to do? I call down to Adrian's office but Angie tells me he is still exiting Michelle. My only option left is for me to pack up his stuff myself. I take his suitcase out of the cupboard and pack up all his clothes. I fill his laundry bag with his toiletries and shove them all into his suitcase. I pack up his books, his newspapers and his car magazines. Then I drag the whole lot downstairs.

Liz is horrified when I tell her what I have done. Fortunately, she gets distracted by the arrival of the late-checkout man who is accusing the hotel of theft.

For a guest in an expensive five-star hotel, he doesn't look very pleasant: his hair needs brushing, his suit needs cleaning, and his face is still greasy with sleep.

"Afternoon, sir," says Liz, politely, but on purpose.

"Morning," he replies. "Now," he starts straightaway, "I'd like to report one hundred pounds missing from my bedroom immediately. Where's the manager?"

"I'm sorry to hear that, sir," says Liz. "Are you sure you haven't mislaid it? It is unlikely to have been stolen in the hotel. We simply don't have a theft problem here, sir." That's one of our techniques: always deny that any of the staff could have nicked anything; it is the best policy. Officially, his stuff is in his room at his own risk. We won't take responsibility for anything in the room; valuables should be left in Reception or placed in the safe provided. "Was it in the safe?" she asks. I always ask that one myself; but it does tend to wind them up a bit.

"No, of course, it wasn't in the safe!" he says. His voice is beginning to sound pissed off. "If I knew there were thieves in the hotel, I might have done."

"There are no thieves in the hotel," she says.

"Then how come I'm one hundred quid down, then?" he asks, leaning on the counter.

"What did you do last night, sir?" asks Liz.

"I went out to dinner. I went gambling. I came back," he says.

"Are you sure you didn't use it gambling?" she suggests.

"No. I mean, yes, I'm sure," he says.

"Well, if that's the case, then I suggest that we call the police," she says, picking up the phone.

"D'you know?" says the man suddenly. "I'm too busy for all of this. Just give me my bill and I'll go."

That always happens. I don't know whether he is trying it on, to get some money out of the hotel, which, for the record, we would never give. Or if he did genuinely lose it gambling and forgot. Or even if one of our light-fingered staff lifted it. Either way, mention the police, as we are obliged to do, and everyone from the opportunist to the alcoholic amnesiac always gives in. Eventually, he pays up and pisses off. Housekeeping breathes a sigh of relief: that is one less room they have to worry about.

I check my watch, it's 12:40 P.M. Michelle is taking a long time with her exit. Either that, or perhaps the auditor got in there before her, while she was sitting outside waiting.

Traffic through Reception is beginning to get a little heavy. The lunchtime drinkers are starting to arrive, coming through to have a swift one at the bar before going on into the restaurant.

The people who lunch in an expensive hotel such as this— famous for its modern and traditional cuisines—can usually be split into various groups. Firstly, there are the expense account lunchers: businessmen who work in and around the area and meet up with an important client here for a long, languid, beef on the bone, coffee and liqueurs lunch. Secondly, there are glamorous lunching ladies who regularly meet for flutes of champagne and salad. They tend not to eat or drink too much, but they can often stay quite late into the afternoon, only leaving to collect their children from school. And thirdly, there are the occasion lunchers: people who are in town to see a show, or who are taking Granny out on her eightieth, or young men introducing their fiancée to their parents. They tend to be larger groups of five or six, and they take a long time to order and stay late into the afternoon.

But it is really only the businessmen who go to the bar for a drink first. Gino can tell almost as soon as they stand at the bar and order their first drink, who is going to spend some money and who is not worth being ever so pleasant to. He told me once that the men who come in and order a double straight off mean business. The ones who stand and think about what they should be ordering are not worth chatting up, as they probably won't be hanging around for liqueurs and chocolates later on.

I smile at a couple of likely-looking fat lunchers as they come through, dressed in their smart pinstriped suits, handmade shirts, and red suspenders. I wish them good morning, and I'm concentrating so hard on them that I almost miss Michelle coming through the glass doors.

"Michelle," I say after her, as she tries to sneak past.

"Oh hello," she says, stopping in her tracks.

"You weren't going to leave without saying good-bye, were you?" I ask, sounding offended. I like Michelle. We've worked together for eight months on the desk. She is much better company than Liz. She likes a gossip and a drink and I like that in a girl.

"No," she smiles, glancing around at Tony's desk, waiting for some cheeky comment. But Tony's busy: he's got a client at his desk, some young bloke whom I have seen a couple of times before—a businessman with an office around the corner. He sends quite of few of his Russian clients to the hotel, and he pays Tony five hundred pounds a month in cash, to make sure both he and his guests are well looked after. Tony has a few deals like that going on. But he likes to keep them quiet: there is no telling how the management would react if they found out Tony was moonlighting.

Michelle comes over and stands behind the huge floral arrangement we have on the counter, hoping that Tony won't see her.

Liz is busy on the telephone, snapping small sections off her health bar biscuit as she speaks.

"So how was it?" I ask Michelle.

"A lot better than I thought," she replies. "But he went through everything. All the guest comments that have ever been made about me; all that sort of stuff."

"Really?" I ask. "That's what took you so long? It sounds very thorough."

"It was," she nods. "Maybe he was making up for the Personnel girl being on honeymoon. Anyway," she says. "I suppose I'd better go. You've got work to do."

"Alright?" asks Liz as she puts the phone down.

"Yes, thanks," says Michelle. "You?"

"Very busy," smiles Liz.

"I can see," says Michelle.

"When do you start?" asks Liz.

"In a week. I'm going on holiday before."

"Good," says Liz. "That's nice."

"Spain."

"Good," says Liz. The telephone rings. "See you around," mouths Liz as she picks up.

"I'd better go," says Michelle again.

"I'll walk you to the door," I say.

Michelle walks past Tony's desk and he says nothing. Deep in his meeting with the businessman, Tony wouldn't dream of being unprofessional enough to make a sharp comment, although from the flicker of his eyes as she goes past, you can tell he is gagging to.

Steve opens the door for us as we walk out into the street.

"Bye, Michelle," he says offering her a white-gloved hand. "Good luck."

We walk a little further along the pavement, I kiss Michelle on the cheek and I tell her to keep in touch; she lies and says she will, I do the same. But we both know that the only way I will see her again is if I move to The Savoy. That's the thing about working in hotels, you have almost no time to socialize; most of the time, I'm too exhausted to do anything, so I sit at home alone and watch the telly. I wave to her as she walks up the street. I'm really going to miss her: it's going to be lonely in Reception without her.

I nod towards Steve, who is opening a taxi door; hoping to relieve its occupant of a quid. Steve is good at relieving people of pound coins. Every time he opens a door, every time he hails a cab, every time he carries someone's bag, he gets one. They all sit jangling in his pocket, and by the end of the week, he can have anything from six hundred to a thousand pounds in small golden coins. It's no wonder, then, that plenty of people would quite fancy Steve's job. Even if it does entail standing outside in all weathers, wearing a thick uniformed coat, and being polite to people.

I take the opportunity to walk around the corner to the back of the hotel for a quick cigarette.

The noise coming from the kitchen is off the scale. Chef, it seems, is having a hissy fit because his chicken livers haven't arrived. I can hear him swearing and shouting "livers, livers, livers," from the street. There is steam rising from the open kitchen windows and I can see them all running around in there.

This hour before lunch is always madness. Chef is getting ready to call the orders in. It looks like an easy job but it's not: it has to be the hardest role in the kitchen. He has to stand there and take control of, and command the respect of, some one hundred fifty people. It's like conducting a symphony—everyone has to be on time and with the beat of the kitchen, and if anyone misses their cue, then the whole thing falls apart. It is so difficult and so stressful, especially when people fuck up, which they do all the time. There is a real art to it, and God, does Chef scream when you get it wrong! Then there are the *sous*-chefs to contend with, who buzz around like blue-arsed flies. The *chefs de partie*, heads of sections, in charge of the grill or vegetables, are always quite anxious, as they have a lot to manage. Then there are the first commis chefs, who have been in the kitchen for about two years (and they're doing all right for themselves on fourteen thousand pounds for a forty-hour week, though they end up working eighty) but they are still likely to make mistakes. Then there's the second commis chefs, who are about eighteen or nineteen. They're trainees, like I used to be, who know nothing and are there to be shat on. And then, finally, there are the porters. Altogether, it is a vast team, working with vast quantities of food, hectic, with a hell of a lot of work to be done. The pressure is high, you are working against the clock, there is no slacking allowed, so you can understand why it is always a little hysterical just before the lunchtime rush begins.

I stub out my cigarette just as there is a cheer of delight from the kitchen as a delivery of chickens livers finally makes it through the door. I walk around to the front of the hotel and see Tony just finishing up with his businessman. He has a wide grin on his face and a large brown envelope of cash, presumably, in his inside coat pocket. Liz beckons me over quickly, her nylon nails working overtime.

"There you are," she says. "I've been paging you—I'm desperate for a toilet break, and the phone keeps on ringing."

"Oh, I'm sorry," I say, taking the small red pager out of my pocket. "I've forgotten to turn it on."

"Really?" She rolls her eyes.

"Leave it to me," I say, getting back behind the desk. "You take as long as you like," I add, thinking I might just give Ben a quick call while she's gone, to give him a Michelle update. But the phone rings again, before I have the chance. It's Jackie.

"Hi," she says. "I was just wondering if you could send Ben up to check out a room for me. Number 407 really needs inspecting."

"It really needs inspecting?"

"Yes," she says.

"Well, I'm afraid Ben won't be here until later. He's on nights this week."

"Oh, of course he is."

"But I could come up in a minute, and help you out," I suggest.

"Don't worry," she replies quickly. "I'll do it myself." She hangs up.

I start to laugh. "She's outrageous," I say.

"What?" says Tony, whose bat-like hearing is always tuned in for gossip.

"That Jackie."

"She wasn't ringing up for a shag again, was she?" smirks Tony.

"How do you know? I thought it was supposed to be a secret."

"As you should know by now, there are no secrets in hotels. If there are any secrets, it's my job to know them. And anyway, she's done it before," he says. "Ben isn't the first handsome bloke on Reception who's been through Jackie's laundry basket."

"No!" I say, my mouth hanging open. I'm so naïve.

"'Fraid so," says Tony with a click of his teeth, firing off a quick shot with his right index finger. "I think you'll find she's very accommodating."

With rumors of the obliging nature of Jackie's laundry basket ringing in my ears, I decided against calling Ben to update him on Michelle's exit. It is bit off-putting to know that Jackie's been there and done that before. Not that Ben's in love with her, mind you. It just makes him out to be a bit of a fool and their whole relationship a bit phoney. Would he mind if he found that he wasn't the first to inspect rooms with Jackie? Is it my duty to tell him, anyway? I don't know. We are friends; he showed me the ropes when I first came here a year and a half ago. Ben's been on Reception for two years now and he seems happy to stay here, while I, on the other hand, really want to make the grade. Maybe, I think, as I gaze into space and ignore the ringing telephone, maybe I'll tell Ben later when he comes in. It depends on what sort of mood he is in.

Liz comes back from her extended toilet break. I don't know

what she's been doing, but she smells very strongly of perfume. Why do women do that? You can tell the guests don't like it, they recoil slightly when she leans on the counter to flirt with them.

The lunchtime rush is now well and truly on. Herds of men in suits keep filing through Reception, the expectation of a fat lunch writ large all over their faces. I know Gino is rattling that cocktail shaker of his, as a serving suggestion to anyone who comes into the bar. There is something about the sound of ice on silver that gets people going, of a lunch hour. He'll be shifting those Bloody Marys like his mother's life depended on it.

Tony's at his desk with another young man who has come in to sell him bicycle tours, if I eavesdrop accurately. He looks a bit lean and keen, something that I know Tony finds very unattractive. It's usually around this time that Tony receives his salesmen: for the next hour or so, people with briefcases and pamphlets will come into and out of the hotel, trying to persuade Tony to take them on board. Tony will ask what his cut will be, and depending on the attractiveness of the offer he hears, you will either be accepted into his little leather folder of delights or you will very politely be asked to go on your way. Needless to say, the bloke with the bicycle is charmingly turned down.

"We have more of a taxi-based clientele," says Tony standing up to shake his hand. "But good luck, mate, it sounds like an interesting idea."

Tony is never rude to anyone useful; he says you never know if you'll need them at a later date, so everyone who meets him thinks they're his new best mate. It's a talent that Tony has in spades. The skinny guy walks out through the door and Tony picks up his *Time Out* magazine. A concierge's bible, it tells him exactly what's on where and keeps him abreast of little details like opening times and curtain-up times. He does also have his copy of the *Golden Keys Journal*, sitting on the desk. Packed with world concierge gossip, it tells him which concierge is doing well and who is moving on in Singapore, or wherever.

Lynette comes rushing around the corner and into the back office behind Reception—she has pages and pages of paper in her hand and looks hassled.

"How's juggling occupancy going?" I ask.

"We're minus ten at the moment," she says, her magnified eyes blinking.

"What, ten rooms overbooked?" I say.

"I know, I know," she says. "But the situation could change at any minute, as you know. I was minus twenty-five two hours ago, just before we went into the manager's meeting."

"Right," I say.

"Who have you checked in? Anyone?" she asks, flicking through all her paper.

"We've had the red-eye guys in, so far, plus the Canadian . . ."

"Oh my God, will you check that someone sent him up a complimentary bottle of champagne to compensate for the mess-up this morning?" she asks.

"Yes, of course."

"Anyone else?" she asks, her pen poised.

"Not yet, Lynette. It's only lunchtime."

"Lunchtime?" she says, sounding confused.

"Yes."

"Oh. I thought it was about 3:00 P.M."

"No."

"Phew!" she says. "I must remember to get some satin sheets put in 505."

"I'll call up if you want?" I suggest.

"Would you?" she asks.

"It's fine."

"They're for the Texan."

"What time is he arriving?" I ask.

"Sometime this afternoon," she says, before rushing off back to the manager's office.

I call up Jackie to make sure that the Texan has the correct sheets in his penthouse bed. Room 505 costs two thousand pounds a night (not including breakfast) and I am sure we will be charging him at least one hundred pounds extra for his satin sheets. The hotel industry loves special requests. At the last place I worked, Madonna turned up, and complained about the exercise bike that we had in the gym, so the hotel ordered a special piece of equipment for her and charged three times the price to her room. Well, she'd been quite difficult already, complaining about the color of the curtains in her room, for example, and we had to move her from suite to suite five or six times. But then again, even Madonna doesn't have a monopoly on difficult. There's a story about Cher's people calling up the St. Martin's Lane hotel to say that she wanted all her food to be organic and from Harrod's. So the hotel went all health-food-mad, shelling out a fortune for her. She also asked for a couple of exercise bikes to be put in her room. They went and emptied the gym, taking everything up to her room. Apparently, Cher then arrived, said something like "This place is a fish bowl," and walked straight out of the hotel.

But when it comes to requests, the weirdest thing was when Michael Jackson stayed at The Lanesborough and asked for a ton of American stuff that all had to be sent over from the States— Hershey bars, jellybeans and Gatorade. I suppose, with Michael, all these things are par for the course. Jackson is the only star I know who brings his own chef with him, only to have him serve up children's food like chicken nuggets, burgers, and fish fingers. Jackson also had his suite turned into an amusement arcade, full of computer games, like Space Invaders. We also put another television in the room so he could have rolling cartoons on all day long. He must be the most overrequesting star I have ever come across. But then again, he was also the most generous towards his fans.

There were always hundreds of fans hanging around outside the hotel. They would sit and chant Michael's name in the vain hope of luring him to the window. The Room Service guys and I used to play a prank sometimes. We would rattle a curtain and then one of us would put on one of our white service gloves, and then, as the screams grew louder and louder, we would give the crowd a little white-gloved wave. They'd go mad. And we would collapse behind the curtain laughing. Once we waved and waved, and we could hear the crowd shouting, "It's him! He's here! He's coming out to see us!" Then one of the boys pushed me out onto the balcony. Five hundred flashbulbs went off. I have never heard such a collective sigh of disappointment as when they realized it was just me.

There was always a hard-core group of fans who set up a proper camp next to the security fencing, with their tents and their sleeping bags, and on cold nights, Michael would send out a hundred cups of hot chocolate for all of them, which I thought was rather kind. No one else ever did that.

Jackie is a bit irritated by my call to check up on the satin sheets. I don't know whether it is because Ben is on nights and she can't get her usual daily service, or that she is genuinely annoyed that I have been told to check up on her. Of course, she has done the pillows and, of course, she has organized the sheets. She is totally aware that the Texan is arriving today, and the room has been arranged accordingly. I hang up on her, rather wishing I hadn't bothered to call.

Meanwhile, Liz is jotting down a message on a piece of paper. "Yes, sir, of course, sir, absolutely, sir," she says. "I'll send someone right away." She hangs up. "You wouldn't take this to a Mr. Maison in the dining room, would you?" she asks, smiling a wide lip-lined smile.

"Right," I say, resigned to the deal. "Do you have any idea what he looks like?"

"Blue shirt, red tie, bald head."

"That'll really narrow it down," I say, picking up the note.

I walk into the Restaurant. Golden chandeliers, high-backed chairs, linen-covered tables, bustling service and bubbling conversation; the place is traditional, packed, and smells delicious. Red wine, truffle oil, roast beef, sizzling grilled fish, their aromas fill the air, and my mouth immediately starts to water. There is something about a good hotel dining room that just exudes decadence. All I need now is the waft of a fat cigar and the scent of leather to remind me of the good old days at The Savoy Grill. That place was amazing. Before its Marcus Wareing makeover, it smelt of old money and Establishment; it was old school at its best. Racks of lamb, beef on the bone, and twenty-four different ways to prepare a potato—from *pomme sables* to *pomme soufflé*.

When I worked there, those really were the days of the big spenders. Roger Moore used to love it there. There was an occasion when he and two other guys came in for lunch. They didn't hold back in the slightest, and by the end of a six-hour session, they had ended up with a bill of forty-five hundred pounds, or about seven thousand dollars, for the three of them. They paid in cash, putting a big pile of notes on the table. So I picked up the money, and then came back twenty minutes later to find another big pile sitting there. The men were all slightly the worse for wear, so I walked up, thinking that they might have been slightly forgetful. "Gentlemen," I said, "you have actually paid the bill." And one of the guys turned around and said, "No, you idiot, that's the tip."

I remember picking up the two-hundred-pound wad, and all the way back to the side of the room, trying, but failing, to work out how to avoid the "tronc" system. This is one of those egalitarian systems where all tips are pooled, and then split among the waitstaff. At The Savoy Grill, you could earn quite a lot of money: I'd get up to four hundred pounds a month in cash. But the headwaiters and the manager were taking home about twenty-five hundred to three thousand pounds cash per month. Service was never included on the bill, and everyone always tipped in cash. The only way around the tronc was to cover the cash in a napkin as you were clearing the table and pocket it. But woe betide you if you got caught.

It was a very interesting place to work. Margaret Thatcher was in there all the time when she was Prime Minister. She was a great whiskey drinker: she was fond of the double whiskeys, and she would always have the same table, Number Four. If you were anyone in The Savoy Grill you would have a banquette table down the side: Tables Four, Five, Six, Seven, or Eight. They were at the far end of the oak-paneled room. It was almost like an old gentleman's drinking club. The tables were enormous, but you would only ever really have two people at each table, and because of high alcove walls, it was very intimate and no one could hear your conversation. So many deals, and affairs, went on there; it was amazing.

The place was so discreet, the Queen Mother was a regular and loved it. When I was working in the kitchen, we would all joke that she needed a stepladder to get to the table, she was so small. But she was actually great. There would be her full security entourage put at one table, and she would hobble in and sit at another. She would always dine late, and only with friends and never with any other members of the Royal family. She would always order off the menu. She really liked simple food; she was mad for fish-and-chips. She drank sweet Veuve Clicquot (which they made especially for her) or a champagne cocktail—a shot of brandy, a sugar lump, and some angostura bitters. She would have a maraschino cherry put on top. She'd follow her drink by her order of fish-and-chips. Then, after lunch, she would have green Chartreuse followed by a yellow Chartreuse. It was hilarious. It was always all systems go in the kitchen, with the chefs slicing the potatoes so that every single chip was the same size and cut to perfection. So she would have fish, chips, and fresh garden peas, not the mushy variety. I swear, she treated The Savoy Grill like an upmarket café.

Princess Diana also loved The Savoy Grill and Claridge's. I remember once I went into the kitchen at The Savoy to collect the half-dozen oysters she'd ordered. One of the chefs, who was opening them up said to me, "I'm going to snog Princess Di." I said, "What are you talking about?" And as he said it, he licked his hand and wiped it across all the oysters, before we served them to her. I didn't really know whether to serve them or not, but I did. The Diana Effect was amazing: people always seemed to go a little crazy around her. I will never forget meeting her; all she has to do was look at you with those amazing blue eyes and you were smitten.

The Queen used to be more of a Claridge's person. In fact, she liked it so much that it used to be known as the Royal family's second home. She used to attend these enormous banquets there with fifteen hundred guests. They were so vast that the banquets would be spread over several rooms. There would be a reception first, with champagne and cocktails; then dinner would be announced and everyone would sit down. But every time the Queen went past, everyone would have to stand up and bow or curtsey. And she would walk past about four or five times an evening. As waiters, we would have to stop what we were doing immediately and get in a line, and bow while she went past. Unfortunately, we'd giggle. I suppose it was like laughing in church:

we knew we were not allowed to, but we just couldn't help ourselves.

The oddest thing I can remember about the Queen is that all
she drank was Campari and orange, which has to be one of the
worst drinks going. Prince Philip, on the other hand, drank
lager, or bitter. When I was working there he was a fan of Rud-
dle's Ale, and a cocktail called a silver bullet—which is Wolf-
schmitt kümmel, gin and lemon juice. It comes in a round
tumbler on ice, and it's lethal.

I love the oddities of the Royals and the celebrities I have
waited on. Kathleen Turner was a great petit fours fan. Every
time she ordered her postprandial coffee at The Savoy Grill, she
would wrap the petit fours in a napkin, put them in her handbag
and then claim she never got any. I caught her doing it once, and
she called me over and said, "You've seen me putting these in my
handbag, haven't you?" And I said, "Yes, madam, I have." And
she said, "You're not going to tell anyone, are you?" And I said,
"No, madam, I'm not." And then I went and got her another
whole big tray of them and put them on her table. She ended up
giving me a fifty-pound tip, which I most definitely didn't put
into the tronc.

Not all famous people are that delightful. In fact, Noel Gallagher has to be one of the rudest people I have ever met. I remember being at The Lanesborough once around Christmastime,
and he had certainly been indulging in some festive spirit. He
and a group of people had been sitting there since lunchtime and
it was about eight-thirty or nine o'clock at night. There were
people queuing for the table. The restaurant manager declined to
serve them any more drinks, saying she needed the table back
for the evening, and she suggested they could retire to the bar.
Gallagher refused to go, saying that it was his table, and he
wasn't moving for anyone. She said fine, she would give them
another half hour. She returned, and asked again if they would

move through to the bar. He then just got up and said, "Do you know what? Fuck off!"

But it's not just celebrities who behave badly; sometimes hotel staff can do the oddest things when they come in contact with the rich and famous. I remember once I was escorting Mariah Carey to her hotel room, when I noticed a maintenance guy, with his trousers down, bare-buttocked, sitting on her toilet. I stood there slack-jawed. I couldn't bloody believe it. Fortunately, Mariah was looking the other way. It was only when I got him out of there that I learned he was a fan and had simply wanted his backside to be close to hers.

Glancing quickly around the room, I see there doesn't seem to be anyone famous in here today. I walk up to André, the Restaurant manager, and ask if there is anyone there that fits the description of Mr. Maison.

"Blue shirt, red tie, bald head," I say.

André is in a panic. He has three tables waiting for main courses, and a waiter who seems determined to get his coffee made for his table for two before serving the main courses, which is pissing the kitchen off no end. André is also so high on caffeine he is sweating and can hardly concentrate. I can't believe the waiters in here are still up to their old tricks.

When I first arrived here, it used to be a standing joke to give André too much coffee. He has a heart problem, so isn't really allowed to drink it, though he allows himself a couple of strong espressos in the morning. But after 11:00 A.M. it is decaf only. But, to be frank for a second, André is a bit of a shit. He is the sort of restaurant manager who removes a fork after you've laid down silver for the whole dining room, and then demands that you check your tables again to see if you notice anything, berating you severely if you don't. So the waiters used to deliberately overcaffeinate him. When he'd ask for his decaffeinated coffee just before service starts, they'd give him a triple espresso in the hope of sending him into the stratosphere. Today, judging by the dank sweat on his white forehead, is clearly one of those stratosphere days. He'll drop down dead one day, and then there'll be a few waiters who might have to ask themselves a few tricky questions.

I spot Mr. Maison over on the other side of the room, lunching with two other bald men in ties. As I approach, I notice they are drinking a red Chateau Palmer, Margaux 1989 (at four hundred fifty pounds, or seven hundred dollars a bottle). They seem to be celebrating something. I hand over the note and Mr. Maison makes great play of fishing his wallet out of his high-waisted trousers. I stand and smile and wait, thinking it would be nice to see a brown note come out of the pocket, but a blue one would be fine. Instead, he fishes out a fifty-pence piece from the depths of his trousers and pats it into my hand. I'm half inclined just to let it fall onto the floor. But I'm broke, and these things all add up over time.

It's relatively quiet on Reception. Liz is loudly sucking on a mint and looking through the passports of some French couple who have just checked in. She smiles as she works out exactly how old the woman is.

"Can you believe she is forty-four?" asks Liz, looking up, her cheeks firmly sucked in, as she gets to grips with her mint.

"Well, I can't say that I saw her properly; they were heading for the elevators when I came out of the Restaurant," I say.

The French couple's bags are still sitting by the front desk in the shiny brass luggage trolley. Neither Jez nor Dave are very keen to take them up to the third floor. For, just as the Americans are feted for their generosity, so the French are famed for their general tightness when it comes to tipping.

They are certainly not unique in the deep-pockets/short-arms department. The Italians are also rubbish, as indeed are the Spanish and the Greeks. The Japanese are generous, and the Russians seem to be so delighted to suddenly have so much money, they can't help splashing or sharing it around. But the most welcome hotel guest has to be the Arab. Even more profligate than the American, the guy from the Gulf spends money like water and drinks rare whiskey like water. I remember a girl in a hotel that I worked in once who was given a first-class return ticket to India for herself and a friend because she had been so helpful to this Saudi. The concierge was a little angry, as he thought he was entitled to a bit more than the five-hundred-pound watch that he'd been given. But that is one of the problems when the really big spenders come into the hotel: everyone starts to get a little greedy. You can almost smell the service seeping back into our industry this afternoon as we are all on tenterhooks, waiting for the Texan to arrive.

I look at my watch and smile. It is about this time that, once again, all hell is breaking loose in the kitchen downstairs, with orders for main courses still coming in and the pastry chef finally proving his tantric worth.

I used to have a mate who was a pastry chef. They are very odd guys indeed, and they're nearly always stoned. Or at least my friend was. They work in a totally different environment from the rest of the kitchen. Their room is cool, to prevent any of the ingredients from melting, and calm, because of the detail and precision of their work. If the head chef is a culinary artist, then the pastry chef is an engraver. Nothing a pastry chef does is loud or flamboyant. The ones I have met are always quiet, introverted, perfectionistic types who can spend hours making a rose out of icing. They can also make baskets out of sugar, and pipe cream into holes you never knew existed. They are largely ignored by the rest of the kitchen, but really come into their own during afternoon tea. Their handiwork is there to be admired on the sweets trolley or dessert menu. Having said that, in a more traditional dining room such as ours, it is usually the more old-fashioned or nursery style of dessert that goes down well, like apple pie, bread-and-butter pudding, or rich chocolate pot. Although we do have various fruits in Grand Marnier, or berries in some sabayon for our more progressive clients.

I decided to go into the back office to check the e-mails. Ewan is often too busy dealing with the faxes and telephone calls to check the e-mail five or six times a day in case something important comes in. I don't mind doing it: it gives me a break from the front desk, although the stale smell of the back room can sometimes put me off. Ewan's on the telephone discussing someone's weekend minibreak in his dull monotone voice. I nod, he nods back. I dial up the server. Five e-mails arrive on the screen. The first two are reservations requests, so I forward them to Lynette's and Ewan's personal in-boxes. The third is junk mail from Ryanair telling us about some flights they have for free. The fourth is some wine company advertising some new South African stuff. And the fifth, headed "Help Needed!" is a little odd.

It is from a woman who appears to be questioning a £10.70 minibar bill that we have sent her. Then, the more closely I read the e-mail, the more I realize that she is not actually questioning the bill, but asking us to change the date of the bill. "I was not supposed to be staying at the hotel at the time of the bill," she says. "And my husband has unfortunately opened and read your letter. And now, as you can imagine, I am in big trouble and I need to find a solution." She goes on to give various e-mail addresses—one her husband can read, and the other he cannot—while she asks us to change the date of the bill and thereby the supposed time of her stay in the hotel. "My marriage depends on your response," she says. "I shall now send you an 'official' request from my other e-mail address about the bill, so that, when you reply, my husband can see the response. I am counting on your readiness to help."

God, I think, as I print off the e-mail, all this hassle over an unpaid orange juice and a bottle of water. Poor woman, the possibility that your marriage will collapse because you didn't own up to those two beverages as you were checking out must be a nightmare. I walk out of the office and share the news with Liz. Liz reads the e-mail three times over, her eyes round, and her mouth half open as she enjoys the drama of it all. She pretends that she remembers the couple in question and starts describing them intimately. I ignore her.

"What do you think we should do?" I ask.

"E-mail her back on husband-mail and say we got it wrong, of course," says Liz, like I was some dumb moron.

"Do you think so?" I say. I am tempted to do as Liz says, but sense there is something fundamentally not quite right about it. And having already made one faux pas already today—packing up a guest's room without his permission—I think I should probably go and ask Adrian. "I think I might go and ask the manager."

"If you really think you can't make a decision on your own," replies Liz, with a dismissive wave of her hand.

"I think it is for the best."

"Right," she says, leafing through some papers on the desk. "Whatever."

I take the printout and walk through the glass swing doors. Ushered into Adrian's office by Angie, I find him at his desk, surrounded by fruit baskets, bottles of champagne, leather wallets, a teddy bear and "Compliments of the Manager" cards. His Mont Blanc pen is poised, as he sits behind his desk signing welcome slips for important guests.

"I'm sorry to bother you, Mr. Thompson," I say, standing by the door.

"Come in, come in," he beckons, his gold cuff link glinting in the sun. "What seems to be the problem?"

I hand him over the e-mail and explain what has happened. He puts down his pen and reads it through, a mild grin of amusement on his face.

"Poor cow," he says. "That must be one of the worst ways to be caught out—over a minibar bill." He laughs. "How tragic is that?"

"So shall I write and say that we got it wrong on her husband's e-mail, then?" I suggest.

"I'm afraid not," says Adrian. "That would technically be fraud," says Adrian. "And if this case should ever come to court and our bill was used as evidence, we would have to lie in court or be caught lying in court. Either way, it is not a good look for the hotel."

"Oh," I say. "It's just that I do feel a bit sorry for the woman, she sounds so desperate."

"I know." He shrugs. "But really for the sake of the hotel, I'm afraid we just can't get involved. Write something along the lines that 'I'm afraid I can't help you with this matter,' and leave it at that. If she writes again, bring it to me, and I will have to write back to her."

"Oh," I say, picking up the printout. "Is that really all we can do?"

"Yup," says Adrian, picking up his pen again. "'Fraid so."

As I turn around to leave his office, there's a knock on the door and Tony walks straight in.

"Tony?" says Adrian.

"Sir," he says. "I think there is some bloke casing the joint."

"Right," says Adrian, sitting up in his chair. "What makes you say that?"

"Well, it's either him, a guest, or a new bloke in Maintenance whom I haven't met yet. Either way, he came into the hotel and took the elevator to the third floor, and then he disappeared."

"Disappeared?" asks Adrian.

"Yeah, well," says Tony, suddenly sounding rather sheepish. "I was talking to a client on the telephone, and it was Liz who noticed him. She says his red baseball cap was pulled a bit low over his face and she suggested that I send Dave up to investigate. By the time Dave got up there, the man had gone."

"Oh," says Adrian, getting up from behind his desk. "Have you informed Mustafa in Security?"

"Yes, first thing I did. He's checking his CCTV screens right now."

"Good," says Adrian. "Because I don't need any paintings going missing. The police have already been in and warned me about a gang that is doing the area at the moment."

Adrian explains that the picture thieves have already done the Cadogan Hotel and Blake's Hotel this week. They apparently brazenly walked into the hotels, took the pictures off the walls in full view of everyone working there, and walked out with them. Everyone in the hotels thought that they were simply a couple of blokes from Maintenance doing their jobs. Blake's had been hit a couple of times before, he says. Last time, a gang walked in and started taking out tables, chairs, glassware, and cutlery, and because they were doing it in such an overt and obvious manner, no one stopped them.

"Do you remember that bloke who stole all those TVs?" says Tony. "From that place, Myhotel?"

"Oh yeah," nods Tony.

A thief had booked himself into two rooms in a new hotel, Myhotel, in Chelsea. All the rooms in the hotel have these state-of-the-art flat-screen computers, on which you can receive e-mails and watch TV. They were amazing, and worth about five grand each. Anyway, the thief sends the concierge up to Harrod's to buy him two computer bags, which, of course, he duly does. Then the thief calmly puts the two TVs into the computer bags and walks straight out of the hotel with them. The hotel tried to track him down but found that he had booked the two rooms on a stolen credit card.

"You've got to be so careful," says Adrian. "Do you remember those five laptops that went from a conference room in The Lanesborough?"

"Yeah," nods Tony. "Hadn't they all gone for lunch? Left the events room unlocked, and when they came back, the place had been filleted?"

"That's right," says Adrian. "Terrible business."

It's not as if the hotel doesn't expect a certain amount of thieving. Ashtrays, teaspoons, bathrobes—they are all factored into the price of the hotel room. But when it comes to things like fridges, toilet seats (two wooden Victorian ones from The Savoy), carpets, and paintings off bedrooms walls, then we start to get annoyed. The ten percent that we add on to the room rates for theft won't cover the gilt chair that is taken down the fire escape and shoved into a van.

"It's not so much the price of replacing the paintings," admits Adrian. "It's the bore of having to find and choose the replacements."

Adrian instructs both Tony and me to keep our eyes peeled around the hotel, and there is another knock on his door. Sally comes in. Dressed in a dark suit with smooth, straight blond hair and two dark blusher triangles on her cheeks, Sally is the glamorous face of the hotel, in charge of PR and sales. She liaises with journalists, hands out free hotels stays, goes to tricky conferences about image and communicating better, but her main job is what is known in the business as "show rounds." She spearheads the hotel's opportunities to pitch for the lucrative weddings, conferences, and cocktail parties. It's her job to take prospective brides around the hotel, gently plying them with champagne as she persuades them to drop something like thirty-five to forty thousand pounds in the hotel on one night. You can see why the hotel is only too happy to lay out a few canapés for the happy couple to taste, or to open a few bottles of champagne in their honor. But it is a stiffly competitive business, and there is normally only one in ten of the brides that Sally shows around that ever chooses to cut her cake in our ballroom.

Afternoons are Sally's busiest time, because she can only really operate when the hotel is quiet. Part of her job is to show various journalists or potential conference clients around the rooms available in the hotel, and for that she needs green-lit (VI), clean, unoccupied rooms—something which is only readily available in the short window between 2:00 P.M. and 3:00 P.M. in the afternoon.

She stands in Adrian's office with a broad grin on her face, looking from me to Tony and then back to the manager.

"You're not still being pleased with yourself for saving tonight's cocktail party from near-disaster, are you?" asks Adrian, taking the lid off his Mont Blanc pen again.

"No," says Sally.

"What, then?'" asks Adrian. "You aren't wanting more plaudits just for doing your job again, are you?"

"Well, a bit," she smiles. "I have just secured us a large wedding for five hundred and fifty guests on a Sunday night!"

"On Dodo Night?" asks Tony.

"Who gets married on a Sunday night?" I ask.

"They're a very nice Jewish couple from North London," says Sally.

"Extremely nice," smiles Adrian. "Well done, Sally."

"I can't believe it," she says. "It was touch and go between us and the Mandarin Oriental. I had to undercut them by a couple of thousand, but we can always make it up in corkage."

Part of the appeal of these large events is the corkage. The hotel can charge you from upwards of ten pounds simply to open a bottle of wine or champagne that you have supplied yourself.

It is amazing: not only does it sting you for opening the alcohol but it also stings you again when you come to pay. Places have been known to turn around and say that you drank forty bottles when in fact you have only drunk thirty-two. I remember a wedding we did recently, where they drank sixty-five bottles of champagne and Adrian charged them for eighty-five. They also drank one hundred twenty bottles of water and we charged them for two hundred. Well, who is going to bother to count? If you're rich enough to drop forty thousand pounds on a wedding, you really aren't the sort of person who is going to go down into the depths of the hotel and start counting up the empties at two in the morning.

The amount of pilfering that goes on has to be seen to be believed. I remember a mate of mine once did a thirty-hour shift at this wedding and he managed to help himself to eight bottles of Dom Perignon. He wrapped them, one at a time, in his tea towel and then took them to his locker downstairs, telling everyone that he was going on a toilet break.

The hotel also loves to rent out its large occasion rooms. It is the easy money: they charge from three hundred pounds upward an hour for a room that would normally be sitting idle. Banqueting, award ceremonies, conferences, and weddings are a win-win situation for any hotel.

Tony and I congratulate Sally as we leave Adrian's office and walk back to Reception. I show Tony my e-mail as we walk along. It is important to include him in the gossip and try to keep him on my side.

Back in Reception, Tony and I stop dead as we come through the glass swing doors. Neither of us really knows where to look. Tony snorts slightly as he tries to get himself together. I dig my fingernails into the palms of my hands as I walk towards the desk.

"Good afternoon, ladies," I say.

Two heavily bandaged heads turn very slowly in my direction. They are both wearing dark glasses and have clearly just come out of the hospital after having their faces lifted.

"Hello," mumbles one of them, and immediately regrets it, wincing in pain.

"Mmm," mutters the other, as she fumbles through her wallet trying to find her credit card.

"Is it four days that you will be staying with us?" asks Liz, checking through her pile of paper.

"Mm," agrees the taller bandaged woman.

"Right," says Liz, talking to them both as if nothing was out of the ordinary at all. "We have put you in adjoining rooms so that you can keep each other company."

"Hmm hm," mutters the taller woman again.

"I'll get Jez to take up your bags for you both. Remember, no bending down for either of you," smiles Liz. "I hope you feel better tomorrow."

The two women walk very slowly towards the elevator. Each and every step appears to cause them pain. We are used to plastic surgery patients in the hotel; they always check in during the early afternoon, after their doctor has given them the all clear on his lunchtime round. But it is still a bit of a shock to the system when they arrive; you don't really know where to look. How are you supposed not to notice when someone has lips like a pantomime duck? What are you supposed to say when a pair of zeppelin breasts walk into Reception half an hour before their owner? The whole thing is a bit mad. As if a pair of shades makes them look any better.

English women tend to come in pairs—two friends undergoing the knife together, like it's an alternative to a fun lunch or something. Foreign women are nearly always nipped and tucked on their own, but they arrive with an entourage that can sometimes include several small children. They all stay three or four days locked up in their rooms, ordering soup from Room Service, and then leave to have their dressings taken off somewhere on Harley Street, before checking out of the hotel as if nothing has happened. Most of the time, they never receive telephone calls or visitors. They leave as incognito as they arrived; ready to present their new face, lips, backsides, and breasts to their amazed and skeptical friends.

"Oh, that looks painful," says Liz as the elevator doors slide shut.

"Like some fucking freak show," smiles Tony, as he sits back down at his desk. "One of them looked like she should of done her backside at the same time. No point in having a face that looks like you're in a permanent state of alarm, if you arse is down by your ankles."

"Shh," says Liz. "They might hear you."

"What, through all that bandaging?" I say, laughing as I pick up the phone.

Liz and I stand at Reception talking about what parts of our bodies we would like to have enlarged, reduced, lifted, tucked, or separated. She starts to point out faults in her appearance that I have simply never ever considered worrying about before. She says that her calves are too fat and she would like some sort of extra shape in her upper arms. These are two body parts I was utterly unaware of until now. She would also like the bags removed from under her eyes. I suggest that the bags come with the job. But, unfortunately, now that she has pointed them out, I tend to agree. She could do with having her lower lids tightened up somewhat. She answers the telephone, and as she smiles and talks someone through switching on the television in their room, her bags are all I can think about.

Suddenly, James comes flouncing through the glass swing

doors. His Hugh Grant hair flops everywhere, as he approaches Reception.

"Hi," he says.

"Hello," I reply.

"Have you seen my caviar man anywhere?" he asks, sounding unusually concerned.

"No, not so far," I say.

"Shit," he says, his fringe falling forward as he lowers his head. "I've got Chef breathing down my neck. Our friend, the Texan, has ordered a bucket-load of the stuff to be on ice in his room when he arrives."

"Oh," I say.

"Yeah," nods James, rolling his eyes. "I, my friend, am in the shit."

"What does he look like?"

"Who?"

"Your caviar dealer."

"I've no idea, but he'll be surly and Slav and possibly a bit grubby-looking. They nearly always are. He's called something like Sergei, or Sasha. I haven't dealt with him before. A mate in the restaurant trade tipped me off about him last week."

"Right," I say.

"Will you keep an eye out for him?"

"Sure."

"I would hang around here myself," he says. "But I've managed to track down some Puligny Montrachet 1980 for a really good price, and I don't want those shits at The Dorchester getting their hands on it."

"Right," I say.

"They're also promising some stuff from 1942."

"Good." I nod. Second World War wine is gold dust these days.

"Yes, it is," says James, swishing back through the glass doors. "It is bloody good."

"I'll call you if I see anyone," I say.

"Cheers," says James. "You're a mate."

As I stand pondering what it must really be like to be one of James's mates, I notice a whole load of kitchen staff file past the front of the hotel. Some are still dressed in their chef's whites with pale blue or check trousers, others are in their jeans, sweaters, and thin coats; all of them hunch their shoulders in the cold and are accompanied by a wisp of cigarette smoke.

The kitchen staff are on their split-shift break, the lucky things. God, what I wouldn't give for a hair-of-the-dog pint right now, or a vodka shot, to keep me going. Those guys have got two hours now which they can call their own, and I can guarantee that most of them are going to the pub.

Well, there's almost no point in going home, is there? When I first started working in the kitchen and had no mates, I did pop home a couple of times before I realized my mistake. I slept all the way there on the tube, dribbling onto my own shoulder with exhaustion, and then, when I finally did get home, I made myself a sandwich, watched some kids TV and then took the tube back, sleeping all the way again. I soon understood there were probably better uses of my time.

So, mostly, I'd go to the pub. It was a good way for me to bond with the group and let off steam. I'd sit there with the rest of the commis chefs and waiters, bitching about what went wrong at lunch, and about who landed us in the shit, due to their incompetence at the grill or something like that. It was a laugh. Six or seven languages on the go at the same time, but somehow we all managed to chat. I used to knock back about two or three pints and half a packet of cigarettes during my break. We'd normally all come back a little lubricated after our time out, but no one ever seemed to notice or mind. And we'd all shove in the mints on the way back to disguise any alcohol on our breath. But if anyone had made a fuss, I think they'd have had a mutiny on their hands. You can't expect a hundred and fifty blokes to work their arses off sixteen hours a day without some sort of respite. Anyway, after half an hour in the boiling hellhole that is the kitchen, we'd have sweated ourselves sober.

There were a few of us who didn't drink at all. They were the ones in the really shitty jobs who normally didn't speak much English and who were sending half their wages home to some country somewhere far away. Either they were too broke to drink, or they were too exhausted. Some of them had other jobs, cleaning somewhere else, and used these two hours to pass out in the staff room, catching up on some shut-eye.

The stoners didn't have much to drink, either. They'd rather have a few joints than pints any day, and they'd sit in the corner of the pub eating crisps, zoning out and going around the corner for tokes. It always used to amaze me how they made it through the next shift: dope makes you tired and wanting to go to bed. I was usually knackered enough before the dinner service, without a joint adding to my problems. I always suspected that they probably supplemented their drug supply a bit later on, adding coke or speed to the mix. Some of them would finish the shift at 11:00 P.M. really quite hyper and high, keen to go on drinking somewhere else; while the rest of us could barely manage to put one foot in front of the other to make it home.

Liz has got her hands on the afternoon mail. She is dividing it up into sections, leafing through, sorting out Tony's weekend jaunt brochures from James's fine wine catalogs. There's an awful lot of the stuff; it seems odd, when most of the bookings are done over the telephone these days, that we still get so much rubbish through the mail. Liz takes the pile into the back office. A naturally nosy person, she likes going through the mail before letting Ewan anywhere near it.

"Fantastic," announces Tony, slamming down his telephone,

evidently satisfied. "That'll be an excellent night out, if ever I've heard of one."

"What?" I say, leaning on the counter. With Liz in the back room, it is a good time to let standards slip for a second.

"That was the PR for Chutney Mary, you know, that curry place in Chelsea."

"Yes," I say. "Never been there myself, but I've heard it's a good place."

"Well," Tony smiles. "They've organized a concierge evening next week and they've asked me to come along. There are thirty of us, all concierges. But they say I can bring a couple of mates along."

I can see both Jez and Dave stiffen with anticipation. Normally, when Tony gets invited to these things, which he does about twice a month, it's a toss-up between the two of them who goes. It is supposed to be part of their training process—their way of finding out where it is good to eat, which one is on its way out, which is worth the trek across town. The last thing you want to do, as a concierge, is to recommend somewhere that is mediocre, especially when the client is dropping two thousand pounds a night in your hotel.

"Sounds good," I say.

"Yeah," he agrees. "It is always good to share notes with some of my mates from other hotels. You get the best stories; it's always nice to hear what's going on in the other places."

"I'm sure," I say.

"Want to come with me?" he asks.

I stand up, slightly shocked. Jez and Dave slacken with rejection. "What, me?" I ask.

"Yeah, you," he says. "It might do you good to have a laugh. It's all free," he adds, as some sort of incentive.

"When is it?" I ask, like I'm the busiest person, with an

agenda, a diary, a social life, or indeed a life or a girlfriend—none of which I've got. I used to have a girlfriend, but she dumped me months ago because I kept on having to do nights, and I haven't got around to getting another one for exactly the same reason.

"Next Thursday."

"Sounds great," I say, getting out my empty diary. "I'll jot it down."

As I'm noting down my date with my new best friend, I suddenly notice a suspicious-looking character wandering around the lobby with a large holdall bag, wearing a red baseball cap pulled down low on his face. He looks suspicious, to say the least. He doesn't have enough purpose in his stride to be a Maintenance man (although sometimes you could be forgiven for pulling them over, they way they stroll about their business). I catch Tony's eye. Quick as terrier, I can see he's onto him—his body is stiff, his eyes are bright, and he's following his every move. The description certainly fits the man who was hanging around earlier. Are those rolled-up paintings in his bag? The only thing that does worry me is he's not making the fastest of exits. Even so, he does look dodgy. But you have to be careful when approaching people in the hotel: they could quite well be guests, and it is more than your job's worth to ask them to open their bags. One could well be a rock star, or some sort of celebrity in a "street" disguise. Winona Ryder used to confuse us all the time. She'd dress up like a man in order to put off the paparazzi when leaving the hotel. So, such people have to be approached with caution. However, Tony seems to be throwing that to the wind as he walks up to the man.

"Excuse me," he says. The man turns around. "Could you open the bag, please?" The man looks shocked. He puts his hand over the bag and shakes his head. "Could you please open the bag, sir," asks Tony again. "It would be better for you in the long run if you were seen to cooperate, son," he says. The man still shakes his head. "Right," announces Tony. Aggressively shoving the man with one hand, he grabs the bag with the other.

"Nooooo!" says the man, as he collapses in a crumpled heap on the floor.

"I did ask politely," says Tony, unzipping the bag. "Oh," he says, as he looks inside.

"What?" I ask, coming out from behind my desk in some-what tardy support.

"Give James a call, will you," he says. "Tell him his caviar man has arrived."

"Oh," I say, stopping midstride.

"Yes, bit embarrassing," says Tony, walking towards the wall. "Sorry, mate," he says, offering the man a hand to stand up.

The caviar man says nothing. He refuses Tony's offer of help and, brushing himself down, he puts his hand out for his bag of caviar.

James is more flustered and flouncy than usual when he rushes out of his back office and into Reception.

"You didn't hit him? You didn't hit him?" he says to Tony. "Please say there was no physical contact? Otherwise, he won't come here again."

Tony denies all knowledge of any contretemps and the caviar man doesn't speak English well enough to contradict him. In a matter of seconds, James has scooped the man up and taken him into his back office for some calming vodka and some gentle be-luga, sevruga, and oscetra dealing.

The hotel will normally buy everything the guy's got. It's not as if it will be difficult to get rid of the stuff in a place like this; the guests spoon it up like blackberry jam. Mr. Texan Oil Baron has ordered a pound for his room already, if I heard correctly earlier. James, I know now, will be doing a bit of a tasting with his silver spoon. When he's spending thousands of the hotel's pounds, he's got to be careful that he's not buying shit. That's one of the problems when dealing with the black market: you have no recourse if you make a mistake. So the caviar man will be in there for a good half hour while James checks the seals on all the jars, opening the occasional odd one just to see they haven't been tampered with. Then Chef will be doling out the fish eggs to anyone that asks for them. We could even get a few takers at tea.

It's ten minutes to four and the tea crowd should turning up soon. I've actually noticed a few tourists coming through into the lounge for tea already. They can cause a few problems sometimes. We're an upmarket, destination, five-star hotel, so we have a no-sneakers, no-shorts policy in our lounge, which can make it rather tricky when it comes to tea. No one likes afternoon tea more than the Americans, and they, no matter what their size, tend to favor shorts and sneakers. So it often ends up being a quid-pro-quo situation. If there's a large group who look like they might spend a lot of money, then we let them in. If it is only a couple who look a little overawed by the place, then I usually tell them to go to the café around the corner.

As with everything in the hotel business, tea is about making money. And there is nothing that a big hotel like ours likes more than afternoon tea. Just think of the markup. The cost for a pot of tea, some cakes and dainty sandwiches, plus a couple of strawberries, scones, and some cream is less than £1. We charge £11.75 per person and £5 extra for another pot of tea. At the last place I worked, it was £28 for a full stand of sandwiches and cakes, which I know for a fact cost them £2 to make.

We don't even make the mini-éclairs or strawberry meringues on premises anymore. Our stoner pastry chef is usually too busy making canapés or mad creations for Banqueting to spend hours making dainty cakes these days. We buy them all: they are delicious, but they're not made here. When our pastry chef does have the time, he can make the most exquisite, beautiful works of art, but nowadays he's only really required to do that sort of stuff for weddings.

Gino also likes to try and get in on tea. It is a good time of day for him to get rid of some flutes of champagne at £10.50 a glass, with less than £2 of cost. Depending on how busy his bar is with post-lunchtime boozers, I have often seen him walk through the lounge carrying a bottle of chilled champagne, by way of a serving suggestion.

Apart from the Japanese and American tourists, for whom an English tea has constant appeal, the tea crowd has changed a bit over the years. It used to have, much like morning coffee, a middle-class-from-the-country feel to it—women, all dressed up for town, taking their godchildren/girlfriends/mothers out to tea. These days, however, it has become rather more glamorous. The ladies who lunch now also do tea, although obviously not on the same day. Since Kate Moss and Sadie Frost were seen sporting cups and saucers at Blake's, we have noticed a big difference in our tea takings, and that's mainly in flutes of champagne. Girl's teas are now big business, and no one is happier than Gino.

But August is the best month in the hotel calendar for afternoon tea. Actually, August is the best month in the hotel calendar for almost everything, as we are obviously rammed with Arabs. And the Arabs love their tea. At the beginning of the month, when they arrive, they will slip the Restaurant manager one hundred pounds or so to make sure that they have sole use of a particular dining table in the restaurant, and an area in the lounge. And then they go mad. Money is of no object whatsoever and there's a real one-upmanship. Their time clocks are totally different from those of the other guests in the hotel. They get up between two and three in the afternoon, and then they come down for breakfast, which is actually afternoon tea. Dressed to the nines, in the most amazing stuff you have ever seen, the women go totally over the top. They meet for tea and try to work out who has got the most expensive jewelry or who is ordering the most. Although we enjoy it all, they can also be rather annoying, because their teas always go on a rather long time. When you want the dining room back at five-thirty for pretheater dinner, they are still hanging around.

The women will go off at around five o'clock, armed with their sack-loads of cash, and go out hardcore shopping, while the men sit around doing a bit of business. Then they all disappear and come back again at nine-thirty or ten for dinner. They all eat enormous amounts, the men are hammering back vodkas while pretending to drink water in front of their wives. They hit the nightclubs and casinos, and strip clubs in Soho, coming back at about three in the morning. In places like The Lanesborough, which has a special Arabic menu for the month of August, they can then go on to order room service.

The last thing that you need around teatime, with nearly all of your kitchen staff on a break, is any sort of rush on. I heard about a smaller hotel in Kensington that was once caught on the hop by London Fashion Week. A quick stiletto-sprint from the Natural History Museum, where most of the shows take place, they were once descended upon by a gaggle of models—Naomi Campbell, Claudia Schiffer, and various other skinny beauties all piled in at once. The restaurant was absolutely dead, then all of a sudden at 3:45 it was heaving with loads of models, ordering Fat Chips, cosmopolitans, Bloody Marys, and champagne. They stayed for forty-five minutes. They came in, ordered, ordered, ordered, paid their bill, and then, bang, they were gone! The restaurant was totaled—glasses everywhere, bowls everywhere, ashtrays brimming over. And then bang, all of a sudden, they were hit again at about 6:15.

The next day, the hotel got a list of when the shows were, so they knew when the "fash pack" were coming. They decided to be prepared. They fried prawn wong tons, they did some chipo-lata sausages in honey and crudités. They made jugs of Bloody Marys and cosmopolitans. They put bottles of champagne on ice. And they didn't even bother setting the restaurant for din-ner; they stripped it all out and left it that way. The models re-turned and cleaned the place out, all except for the crudités, which, bizarrely, no one touched. In two days, they sold ninety-five portions of Fat chips (£2.75) and two hundred glasses of champagne—a remarkable achievement.

I'm leaning against the counter, listening to Tony talk to some restaurant PR person on the telephone, when I notice a large black limousine pulling up outside the hotel. I can tell the man is important, because Steve immediately stands to attention—that man can smell a tip coming half a mile up the road. Steve walks slowly backwards towards the glass door of the hotel and gives the window a little tap with his white gloves. Tony looks up and immediately stops what he is doing. He puts down his telephone and says loudly to Jez and Dave, who are busy packing up lug-gage on the trolley: "Oi, boys, look sharp, our friend the Texan has arrived."

Mr. Masterson's arrival sends a bolt of electricity through the hotel. Anyone who had previously been half asleep, or underperforming, is now suddenly wide awake and on full beam. It is amazing what the smell of big bucks does to a service industry: suddenly, nothing is any trouble, doors that were previously closed are wide open and everyone is so terribly jolly.

Steve is the first off the block. He speedily opens the door of the limousine, greets the guest by name and has the luggage out of the car and into the hotel before Mr. Masterson has managed to button up his camel-colored cashmere coat. Steve receives a twenty-pound note for his diligence, and bows, walking away backwards from Mr. Masterson like he was royalty. Which, in hotel terms, he is.

Next to give Mr. Masterson the full wattage of his bright smile is Tony. Out of his seat, his hand out in meet-and-greet mode, Tony welcomes Mr. Masterson back to the hotel and asks him about his flight. It is not strictly his role to do that, it's more Adrian's territory, but he earns fifty pounds for doing so.

In fact, as word spreads through the hotel of Mr. Masterson's arrival, everyone comes out of the woodwork. James escorts his caviar man to the door and "bumps" into Mr. Masterson as he is checking in, mentions he's sourced his Trinidad Diplomatic cigars, and earns himself fifty pounds as he does so. Gino pops out from behind his bar, leaving the auditor for one second, to tell Mr. Masterson about the arrival of a delicious special whiskey he might want to try. Gino gets two fifty-pound notes for his trouble. Even André, the caffeine-fueled Restaurant manager, finds a reason to be in Reception when he really should be finishing up the teas. He reminds Mr. Masterson that he has saved him his usual table and gets fifty pounds for his pains. Lastly, Adrian comes out from the back office. Expansive smile and full-on service-industry charm at his disposal, he greets the Texan as if he is his oldest friend in the whole wide world. They shake hands and slap backs, inquiring after each other's health like they both care. Adrian only reserves this sort of welcome for guests who spend more than £10,000 a pop in the hotel. God only knows how exuberant he would have been towards David Beckham and his £433,157 bill at the Hotel Santo Mauro in Madrid.

I let Liz check Mr. Masterson in. I think being surrounded by so much toadying and obsequious commercialism is enough to put anyone off. I don't know why I'm surprised by everyone's reaction: they have been talking of nothing else other than this man and his vast wealth for days now. Anyway, Liz surpasses herself. Flicking her hair, thrusting her cleavage forward, she flirts with him like he is some drop-dead-handsome movie star instead of a short, bald, florid seventy-year-old man. But he seems to enjoy it, and hands over another pink fifty-pound note as he collects his room key. The man has handed out nearly five hundred pounds within five minutes of arriving, and he hasn't yet made it to the elevator.

Jez and Dave both fight for the pleasure of taking Mr. Masterson's luggage to his room. They have one small Louis Vuitton suitcase each. For a very rich man, Mr. Masterson seems to like to travel very light.

"Enjoy your stay," I say to him on autopilot, as he walks past.

"Oh, I didn't see you there," he says, sounding a little surprised. "That's very kind of you," he says, slipping a twenty-pound note onto the desk.

I am a little mortified; the stand that I was trying to take, differing myself from all the other sycophants, hasn't actually gone according to plan. I now look just as bad as the rest of them.

"No, honestly, there is no need," I say, pushing it back towards him.

"Really, son," drawls Mr. Masterson, already halfway towards the elevator. "Take it. There is plenty more where that came from."

"Um, thank you, sir," I say.

"Thanking you," he replies.

As the elevator door closes behind him, an explosion of chatter begins. The lobby sounds like an excited school playground with phrases like "Can you believe it!" "Pink notes," and "Amazing" being bandied about all over the place. The energy level of the whole establishment seems to have doubled with the arrival of one person.

"Well, I thought he was charming," says Liz, flicking her blond hair and clicking nylon nails.

"You would," I say. "I'm going outside for a cigarette."

I don't wait to hear her response. I walk outside the front of the building. We're not normally allowed to smoke outside the front of the hotel, as it is not good for the image of such a smart establishment. You can imagine a whole group of waiters wading around in old butts not being the most attractive of things for an arriving guest. But I'm not really in the mood to care. It's odd, because usually I'd have been all over the Texan like herpes, but today all this fawning has given me a headache. Perhaps I'm more upset about Michelle leaving than I care to think about. We were quite good mates and the idea of endless shifts with Liz brings me down. Or perhaps it's the fact that I toasted Michelle's departure a bit too enthusiastically last night that is making me feel so morose.

I sidle up to Steve, who is stamping his feet with the cold. It's already quite dark outside, and he has got another four hours of standing out here, opening doors and being polite.

"Alright?" I ask.

"Great." He nods, his thick nose all red and running with cold. How he stands it out here in all weathers, I'll never know.

We've got four doormen who work for the hotel: Graham, Derek, Steve, and Dennis. Steve and Dennis are cousins; it's the old keeping-the-job-in-the-family idea at work again. Dennis has been at it for seven years, Derek for five, and the other two are relatively new additions to the fold. But then again, everyone is relatively new in comparison to Steve. Steve's been standing out here for thirty years. Working four days on, four days off, he does a twelve-hour shift from 8:00 A.M. to 8:00 P.M., opening doors and keeping the front of the house clean and respectable. He officially earns eleven thousand pounds a year, although, with all those pound coins he collects, you can multiply that by five. He has become so much a part of the furniture that some of our regulars buy him little presents when they come to stay. His welcoming face is part of the traditional continuity of the hotel. He makes them feel welcome when they arrive, and sometimes he even uses their name when he opens the door, making them feel grand and important in an instant. Little do they really know that he is a moody bastard who drinks like a fish on his days off. The massive broken veins that branch across his thick nose are less to do with exposure to the elements and more to do with nights at home with a bottle of whiskey. But he doesn't seem too bad-tempered today. Perhaps it is the twenty-pound note burning a hole in his pocket that has lightened his mood, or the fact that he has done his four days already this week and in three hours' time, he'll be on a four-day break. He even strikes up a conversation.

"You all right?" he sniffs.

"Been better," I say.

"Going to miss your friend?" he asks, stamping from one foot to the other.

"Who's that?"

"Michelle," he says.

"Yeah," I nod. "More than I'd thought, actually."

"She was quite sexy."

"I didn't think you'd noticed."

"Yeah, well," he says, a chapped smile breaking across his red face. "I see more than any of you lot ever give me credit for. You all think that Tony is the eyes and ears of this place. But you're wrong: I see every coming and going from here, and just because my back is turned to Reception most of the time doesn't mean I'm ignorant of what is going on."

"Right," I say, taking a drag of my cigarette.

"I know about Ben and Jackie in Housekeeping as well," he says.

"Right."

"I know," he says, tapping the side of his nose with his gloved hand, "that shocked you."

"Well, it has a little, as it happens."

"Yeah," he says, as he turns towards a cab pulling up outside the hotel. He smiles as he walks towards the door. "Oi," he says turning quickly around to face me. "Don't stub that bastard out here. Take it with you," he adds, pointing to my cigarette.

I pick my butt off the pavement, and follow the guest slowly in through the revolving doors. Fortunately, from a smoking receptionist's point of view, the guest is Mrs. Robertson, bless her. A dear old biddy in her late eighties, Mrs. Robertson has been living in the hotel since her husband died two-and-a-half years ago. She is sweet, charming, reasonably chatty, but sadly, almost as deaf as a post.

She's so deaf, in fact, that we've had to devise this special method of getting Room Service into her room. She has a room on the top floor of the hotel with a nice view over London that she likes to gaze out on occasionally, in between watching the horses on the telly. For the first year of her stay, her racing addiction was a nightmare. She used to have her TV on so loud that whenever we brought up her morning tea, or any other of her meals, she would never hear any of the Room Service guys knocking on her door. We're not allowed to knock and enter rooms unless we have been invited in. So the Room Service boys would stand outside her room, rapping on her door for hours at a time, Reception would be calling madly on the telephone, and she wouldn't hear a thing.

So Tony came up with this idea. Through a mate of his, he sourced a remote control for the television that we could keep outside her bedroom door, and anytime anyone wanted to get Mrs. Robertson's attention, we'd turn down her volume through the gap under the door. She, of course, was thrilled with the idea and everyone else was relieved.

"Good afternoon, Mrs. Robertson," I say, as I overtake her on the way to Reception.

"What?" she says, turning her small wrinkled face towards me.

I have to say I'm a bit fond of the old dear. I lost my last grandmother a couple of years back and Mrs. Robertson sort of reminds me of her. I like the way she always wears a proper hat and a pair of gloves when she leaves the hotel. There are not many people around who still do that.

But then again, she's quite popular with most members of staff in the hotel, mainly because she is always polite and not much trouble. There was another old lady at one of the places I worked, who was mean and cantankerous and used to urinate all over her chair. We eventually had to put plastic covers on all her seating and add rubber sheeting to her bed. But it in the end, she had to go. She was treating the place like a nursing home and there was no one really qualified to look after her.

On the whole, there is an ambivalent attitude towards long-termers in the hotel business. You would have thought that we would be only too delighted to have guaranteed occupancy of rooms for a great length of time, but it can be a right pain. For a start, it is not all little old ladies wanting their afternoon tea and a biscuit in front of the telly. There are plenty of long-termers who are foreign businessmen that have been placed here by their bank or some other wealthy employer. Stuck in a hotel for two months while trying to find somewhere to live, they become demanding; treating the place like their home, they develop regular affectations like a raspberry-only breakfast, or start wanting the concierge to organize their lives even when the guests are in their office, booking flights and taxis all the time. They want their hotel room to be treated like an apartment, which means that the maids get little or no access, yet they complain when the room has not been cleaned.

We do also get guests who are having their flats or houses refurbished, who check into the hotel for months at a time. They are difficult customers mainly because they're stressed and money is tight, so they tend to never order room service and bring their own alcohol into their room. Long-stayers usually get a monthly invoice, and it is always the house refurbisher who complains about his bill, going through it with a fine-toothed comb.

There are some who prefer to pay in advance instead of the monthly invoice; we take a lump sum off their card and then inform them when it has run out. Mrs. Robertson is the advanced-credit card type. The hotel usually favors advanced payment for the elderly, for obvious reasons.

There is, however, one type of long-term stayer the hotel can't get enough of, and that's the millionaire who likes to keep an apartment in the hotel that he will visit once or twice a year. He'll pay for use of the room for a whole year in advance, on the understanding that it is kept empty, awaiting his whimsical arrival. Except, of course, it is not. I remember the terrible story I heard once about Kerry Packer turning up at The Savoy only to find he could not get into his room. He had a suite there that he rents for 365 days a year and only uses for three or fours weeks maximum. He turned up unannounced one afternoon to stay in his suite, and the hotel had rented it out to someone else. While Reception delayed him, saying there had been a leak in the suite and they were just sorting it out, a whole load of people were dispatched to take all the other guest's stuff out of the room. Packer apparently sensed what was going on and threatened to take his business elsewhere if he didn't get into his room within the next ten minutes. They managed to pull it off. I have no idea how they explained the upheaval to the other guest. The man would have been in an expensive suite. They must have made his whole stay complimentary and apologized profusely for the rest.

"Good afternoon," I say again to Mrs. Robertson.

"Oh yes." She nods finally, after lip-reading my question. "I had a lovely lunch with my grandson at Simpsons-in-the-Strand."

"Good," I say.

"Jolly good," she replies.

"Would you like your room key?"

My voice is bellowing throughout Reception, and Tony is looking a little annoyed. This is one of the busiest times of day for him: he has to confirm all the tables he has booked at various restaurants around London. If he can't fill his tables tonight, he must let the establishments know, so that they can pass the tables on to others further down the food chain. It is also around this time that guests in the hotel start ringing him up, asking him to book restaurant tables. Tony is in one of his terrible catch-22 situations. Should he release his table at The Ivy or Sheekey's and risk getting a telephone call in the next ten minutes asking for a restaurant table? Or should he hang on and risk pissing off the maitre d', who will be less inclined to do him a favor on another occasion? These are the sorts of decisions that determine a good concierge, the sort of concierge other hotels want to poach, which is a practice that goes on all the time. There was someone sniffing around only the other day. Tony, of course, reported it to Adrian, who immediately gave him a pay raise. Good concierges are hard to come by and a luxury hotel always wants to hold on to them.

Mrs. Robertson hasn't heard my last question, but I go to get her key card anyway. The flash of Tony's eyes is enough to make me think twice about asking her again.

"What's got his goat?" asks Liz, looking up from a calculator. She is desperately trying to balance the front register—a job I take great pleasure in delegating, given half the chance.

"Dunno," I say, handing over Mrs. Robertson's key card.

"Don't tell me they've run out of circle tickets for *The Mousetrap*," says Liz.

"Yeah." I laugh. "Or there's been a rush on at *We Will Rock You!*"

"You two can piss off," stage-whispers Tony, as he puts down the telephone.

"I heard that," announces Mrs. Robertson, standing by the elevator.

"How the hell—?" mouths Tony, as she turns to get into the elevator.

Both Liz and I shrug. Tony's telephone rings again. From the whiteness of his smile, I guess it must be an important client. Liz gets back to balancing the daily float accounting for all the outgoing items, like pregnancy-testing kits, that we have had to pay for today. I decide to give Housekeeping a quick call, just to make sure that all the rooms are back and ready for business, before the early evening check-in rush. While Jackie yawns into my ear, complaining about a broken lamp in Room 240, Jenny, the flower girl arrives.

Blond and bubbly, with a flamboyant pashmina draped over her shoulder, Jenny turns up at various intervals in the week to replace all the flowers in the hotel. She does bedrooms on Mondays, common areas on Wednesdays, and the main reception, dining and bar areas on Fridays. Flowers may sound like a trifle, when it comes to the main business of running a hotel, but they are really quite important. They set the tone of the place and are significant enough for a place like the Covent Garden Hotel to spend four thousand pounds on blooms a month, and for a medium-sized place like ours, a monthly florist's bill comes to three thousand pounds. It's a nice little contract, if you can get it. You can also triple your money if you get bookings for banquets or weddings.

Jenny's been through her country-bunch phase, and seems a bit keen on all those tropical flowers at the moment. All fleshy glamour and no smell, I have to say I'm not that fond of them. But then, I only have to work next to the things all week, so who is going to ask me my opinion?

She usually arrives with the arrangement already done, bringing them out of her small minivan that she parks outside the front, with specific instructions for Steve to look out for traffic wardens. She then spends the next ten minutes tweaking her flowers in situ, while talking about her two children to Liz. I swear, I know more about her goddamn family than I do about my own. Her two are in bed with the flu at the moment and Liz, for some reason, moans in sympathy. I move up to the other end of Reception to get away from their chat. I've only got another couple of hours to go and I'm beginning to feel the lateness of last night's party. All I fancy is an early night with some soup, sitting on my sofa.

"Shit!" announces Tony very loudly and very unprofessionally.

"Language," says Jenny, turning around.

"Pardon me," says Tony with a tight smile. "But you might be a little pissed off if you'd just cancelled all your tables at The Ivy only to have the most important guest in the hotel call up and ask for a table for six."

"Oh dear," says Jenny, tweaking some fleshy red thing with a white stamen that looks like a satellite dish.

"Not Masterson?" I ask.

Tony nods, and puts his head in his hands.

No amount of gorging himself on humble pie is going to help Tony out of his situation. He held on to his tables at The Ivy for as long he thought was humanly possible, and now he is in the shit. I can hear him whispering down the telephone. His head is low, as he talks into his chest—he always does this when he is trying to cut some sort of deal. But from his constant scratching of his forehead, I can tell it's not working. He puts the phone down slowly and stares into the middle distance, obviously trying to think.

Liz and Jenny finish talking about Jenny's children and Jenny walks through the glass doors, one orange arrangement in her right hand and a bowl of green leaves in her left, on her way toward the bar. As she walks though the doors, Gino comes bursting out.

"Bloody hell fuck!" he says, walking towards Reception, only to collapse onto the desk in dramatic exhaustion. "Do you know?" he announces, rolling his eyes. "There are times in one's life when one is allowed to kill someone and mine is here. Oh my God," he exhales. "That little shit of a stocktaker, I swear to fucking God he is counting my bloody olives! One, two, three. . . ." His pinched fingers pluck imaginary olives out of an imaginary bowl.

"What?" squeals Liz, leaning over. "Literally, really, going through them all!"

"Nooo, stupid!" says Gino, his eyes rolling again. "But he may as well bloody hell be!"

"Oh, right," Liz says quickly, putting her head down, suddenly very interested in a pile of paper in front of her.

"Really," says Gino, shaking his head. "We are three bottles of Britvic orange short, a bottle of vodka down, and someone has half-fucking-inched a Baileys. Really," he says again, his hands together pleading. "Who fucking cares?"

"There is a Bombay Sapphire thief in the hotel," states Liz, her lined lips pursed.

"We all know that, sweetheart." Gino smiles. "But that's in the maids' bloody department, not with me! I don't sell miniatures, now, do I?"

"I was just saying," says Liz.

"Say away," says Gino with a flick of his wrist. "But it has nothing to do with me."

As Gino leans on the desk bemoaning his auditing fate, Adrian walks brusquely through the glass doors.

"Oi, Gino," he says with a click of his fingers. Gino stands to attention. "What are you doing in your morning suit?" asks Adrian. "It's gone five," he adds, tapping the face of his expensive gold watch. "Black tie."

"I'm on my way," says Gino, theatrically. "I'm just recovering from my stocktaking."

"Now!" barks Adrian, refusing to be drawn into his head barman's dramatics. Gino immediately shuffles off. "Right, Tony," continues Adrian, without breaking his stride. "What's this I hear about Masterson and The Ivy? I've just got off the phone with him."

Adrian parks half a buttock on Tony's desk and sits looking down on him, talking in hushed tones. Tony looks up Adrian's nose for a while, but then turns his face towards his desk and nods continuously. Neither Liz nor I can hear what they are saying. We both lean forward, straining to hear, but to no avail.

After a couple of minutes, my attention is distracted by the return of the kitchen staff, as they file past the front of the hotel after their break. Fortunately, Adrian's back is turned, as, even from here, I can tell some of them are pissed. It's the way they are walking, laughing and slapping each other on the back as they come around the corner. No one could ever be that pleased to be going back down into the kitchens, unless they were drunk. One of the *sous*-chefs runs up to the front window and presses himself against it kissing and smearing the glass. For one dreadful second, I think he is going to moon, bearing his backside to Reception, but I see he spots Adrian's back and he runs swiftly back to join the group.

You can't really blame them for wanting to soften the blow of the next five hours. I always did think that the evening run was worse than the morning. You change into your fresh set of whites and immediately the hell begins. For not only are people tired and tempers fraying, but the stress level always triples as there is so much more to do. Firstly, you've usually got a whole lot of canapés to make as soon as you get back down there. We've got a party for four hundred starting at 6:30 P.M. so God knows how many smoked salmon rolls and blinis they're going to have to churn out before the night is out. There's also a whole load of savory *amuse-bouches* to get ready for the bar. Luxury hotels always run the sort of bars where crisps, peanuts, and the odd green olive quite frankly don't cut the mustard. One of the ways to justify a fifteen-pound martini is to have plates of creamed and piped anchovies on savory biscuits, half quail eggs with lumps of caviar, and prawns on small pieces of toast standing by. All these things have to be made, even before the *sous*-chefs get around to sorting out their *mise en place* for the dinner shift, chopping their parsley, slicing their vegetables. I give one of the commis chefs a little wave on his way and thank God that I am above stairs these days.

Adrian suddenly gets up from Tony's desk and, patting him on the shoulder, says something along the lines that he is glad that something is sorted out. Tony looks relieved. Adrian is a little tense-faced as he walks towards Reception.

"Everything all right here?" he asks.

"Fine," says Liz, her voice sounding oddly high.

"Whose luggage is that?" he asks, pointing to the bag that I'd packed earlier, that is still sitting behind Reception.

"A guest's," I say swiftly, suddenly feeling really quite sick. I'd quite forgotten my early room-clearing. I feel my face go pink, and I wonder if Adrian will notice.

"Well, put it away in the back office. It's untidy. Anyway," he adds, looking at his watch. "When are they coming to collect it? You know we don't like to keep checked-out luggage this long."

"Yes, Mr. Thompson." I bend down to pick up the bag, avoiding all eye contact.

"When's he coming, then?"

"Um, soon," I say, hopefully.

"Good," says Adrian, starting back towards the glass doors. "Stocktaker gone yet?"

"Um, not as far as I know."

"You're on Reception. Is that a yes, or a no?" he asks, dryly.

"No," I say as determinedly as I can.

"Good," he says. "Pay attention." He turns around and points two fingers at his own eyes. "Keep them open."

"Yes, Mr. Thompson," I say, as he turns and walks back through the glass doors.

Everyone exhales as he goes; the tension dissipates, even Jez and Dave were looking a little uptight with Adrian around.

"He's on the warpath," says Liz, ever one to point out the obvious. "I wonder what got up his nose?"

"I've got no idea," I say. "But I can't stand it when he's like that. You alright over there, Tony?"

"Yeah, fine," he says, picking up the telephone. "We're sending the Yank to Sheekey's. I pulled a few strings and Adrian's going to call up and tell him it's a far better place, where you get a better class of celebrity."

"Right." I nod. "No Posh & Beck's."

"Yeah. That was a close call."

A rather attractive redhead walks into the hotel. She looks hassled and wet: it must have started raining outside. She is carrying a whole load of small bags, including a couple of carriers that look like they're doubling as suitcases.

"Hi, hi," she says, as she arrives at the front desk. "Vanessa, Vanessa O'Neil." She smiles, dropping all her bags at her feet.

"Good evening, madam," I say, typing her name into the computer.

She leans on the desk and smiles. I smile back.

"Two nights," she says.

"Right." I say, tapping away.

We both fall silent, and I slowly start to become aware of this odd buzzing sound.

"What's that noise?" asks Liz, coming over.

"No idea," I say, leaning forward on the counter, moving closer towards the source.

Jez, who is walking towards the front desk with a view to

taking Ms. O'Neil's luggage up to her room, stops dead in his tracks, stares at the floor and turns bright red. Ms. O'Neil seems oblivious to the noise, and carries on looking through her handbag for her credit card.

"Room 460," I say, handing over the key.

"Thank you." She hands over her credit card.

The buzzing noise continues, and eventually Ms. O'Neil starts to look around, wondering where it is coming from. Suddenly, Jez kneels down and picks something off the floor.

"Madam," he stutters, great patches of red spreading across his cheek. "I think this is yours," he says, eyes down at the floor, as he hands over a big, black, buzzing dildo.

"Oh my God!" squeals Ms. O'Neil, as she takes hold of the thing, and frantically starts trying to turn it off. Twisting and turning it in her increasingly hot, sweaty hands, she looks like she is about to cry with embarrassment. Eventually, she just opens her handbag and shoves the still-buzzing dildo inside. "Um," she says, turning to face me.

"Yes, madam," I reply. I am so firmly biting the inside of my cheek, I'm convinced I'm about to draw blood. We both stare at each other, both pretending not to notice that her handbag is vibrating.

"Do you mind if I go straight to my room and deal with the paperwork a little later?" she asks, with slow determination.

"No, not at all," I manage to say somehow, through my nose.

Ms. O'Neil gathers all her bags together, refusing Jez's tentative offers of assistance, and runs towards the elevator. You could almost hear the sigh of relief emanating from the poor woman as she collapses against the back elevator wall.

The door closes, and I start to laugh, mainly because I haven't been allowed to. The embarrassment of it all is overpowering. Jez is so shocked, he simply walks slowly around the corner to share his sex-toy experience with Dave. Liz announces that she feels sorry for the woman, and adds that there is nothing wrong with a woman-of-today having a vibrator. Tony thinks it's the best thing that has happened in the hotel all day. He rings his mate at Claridge's to tell him the story; he recounts the whole thing with his fist in his mouth, embellishing as he goes. I can hear the chuckles from here.

Not that Ms. O'Neil's big black vibrator compares to half the stuff the chambermaids find in some of the bedrooms. In fact, there are usually a few surprises about now, as they start doing the rounds turning down the beds in the rooms.

I always think that turndown is one of the most pointless things chambermaids have to do. For starters, most of the guests are in their hotel rooms around this time, having baths, unpacking, or chilling out watching TV, so the last thing they want is to be disturbed by anyone. Least of all, someone who is pottering around their room, doing a whole load of pointless things that they are quite capable of doing themselves. Quite why you need your bed folded back to a ninety-degree angle is anyone's guess. I also love the way, in this hotel, the radio is turned low to jazz on FM and the bedside lamps are turned on, just in case anyone couldn't come up with that suggestion all on their own. The breakfast slip is placed on the pillow, and the remote control put in the corner of the folded sheet. The bedcover is removed and put in the cupboard. And then the final touch is the complimentary bottle of mineral water from the management and any leather wallet or other gifts, and, of course, the chocolates on the pillow.

Pillow chocolates must be one of the few things that the luxury hotel shells out on for little, or no, reward. The truffles we hand out in this place cost £3.50 a box. They are quality stuff, expensively priced and we hand them out for free, every night.

When I say free, I am using that term loosely. If you were to do a financial breakdown on one of our hotel rooms, working out how much it actually costs to turn it around on a daily basis, you would be amazed at how cheap it actually is. It is under £10 per room per day. And that price includes cleaning the sheets, and fresh towels every day (£2.95); newspapers (65p); heating, lighting, wear and tear, theft (£1.10); the wages for the chambermaid who cleans the room (£1.25), as well as the cost of the products she uses to clean (39p); with the Penhaligon's guest supplies (£1.60); and of course, the most expensive outlay of all, the pillow chocolates themselves (£3.50). Knowing this, how we can get away with charging £2,000 a suite a night is quite beyond me.

With Tony still talking sex toys on the telephone, Liz suddenly announces that she is going to staff supper. I suppose, with only a ten-minute break during her shift so far, plus a meager diet bar for lunch, I can't begrudge her her macaroni cheese and bread roll with the rest of them.

She walks off downstairs while I check in a middle-aged couple from Bolton who have a whole sale-of-the-century collection of Louis Vuitton bags at their feet. They range from a family-size suitcase right through to a small vanity case. They seemed to have packed a lot for a weekend. The woman is all excited; she tells me three times that she is going to see a show. Her husband is less thrilled; he sighs as he fills in the form and hands over his credit card. He seems resigned to the fact that this weekend minibreak in the capital is going to set him back at least a grand in hotel expenses alone.

It's just over an hour until I can go home. I lean on the desk, thinking about Friday night TV, possibly a takeout with my Texan twenty pounds and a nice early night. I can't wait. Just a few more check-ins to go. I stare out through the windows and notice the small white dry cleaning van pull up outside the hotel. My heart sinks: dry cleaning is a nightmare. Not only are they always late, but they always, without fail, lose something. The hotel has tried numerous companies—some local, some well known and in prestigious parts of town—and the result is always the same: complaints and lost clothes. It is a service that the hotel is, I suppose, obliged to provide; some of the large ones actually do it in house. But unless you are staying for a length of time, I would advise that you avoid any hotel dry cleaning service.

"Afternoon," says the dry cleaning bloke, as he walks in, dressed in a blue coverall, carrying a pile of white cardboard boxes that look like they should house cakes rather than folded shirts. They're clearly all style over content, this lot.

"Evening," I say, making sure that he knows that I know he is late. The dry cleaning should really be here at about four o'clock, so that Housekeeping has a chance to get into guests' bedrooms in good time should they need it that evening.

He comes back and forth a couple more times, bringing in a cellophane-clad red coat, and what look like some smart cocktail dresses. "That's your lot," he says, handing me over a clipboard to sign. "It's all here," he says, as I start ticking each item off.

"I'm sure it is. I've just got to make sure." I go down the list and it's predictably not all there. "We've got a couple of things missing."

"Not missing. Just arriving tomorrow."

"Right," I say, sounding dubious.

"It's all kosher."

"OK," I say, signing the bottom. "And try not to be late tomorrow."

"Right you are." He takes his clipboard and walks back out to his van.

I call Housekeeping to tell them that the dry cleaning has arrived, but there's no answer. I contemplate paging them, but Dave volunteers to take the dry cleaning around the hotel. He's a bit quick off the mark. Jez is probably still in too much vibrator shock to remember that you can make at least twenty pounds in tips on the dry cleaning run.

Dave has only been gone about five minutes when the telephone calls start coming: someone who sent two shirts in, has only got one back; someone else is missing their tie. Who sends those to be dry cleaned in a hotel? The telephone goes again.

"This is Room 404," comes a female voice.

"Good evening, madam," I say.

"You've lost my two-thousand-pound Valentino dress."

"Oh, right," I say. "I'm sure we haven't lost it, madam."

"Well, I put it to dry clean, and all my stuff has come back except the dress."

"I'm sorry to hear that. I'll make sure you get it tomorrow."

"Tomorrow!" she yelps. "What do you mean tomorrow! I need it now, right now! I have a party to go to in an hour. It is a very important party and I need the dress. I have nothing else to wear."

"Oh." I cover the telephone. "Tony," I whisper, and he looks over. "We've got a dry cleaning problem." Tony nods and gives me a telephone gesture, meaning to pass the call on to him.

"Don't you 'oh' me," says the woman. "I need that dress now. I want that dress right now!" She is beginning to sound understandably hysterical.

"Madam," I say. "I'm terribly sorry, the dry cleaners is closed. We have no way of getting your dress back for you tonight. However, I can personally guarantee that you will get your dress back tomorrow afternoon."

"Afternoon!" she shouts. "I'm checking out at 8:00 A.M. tomorrow morning."

"Then we shall forward it on to you, at our expense."

"Damn right, it is at your bloody expense!" she shouts. "I'll be invoicing you for the room, the dress, dry cleaning, and anything else I fancy."

"I'm very sorry, madam," I say.

"Sorry is not good enough," she says. "I've got nothing to wear tonight."

"I know, madam. And I am just about to forward you to the concierge who can get you any dress you want in town. Don't worry, madam, Tony will look after you. I am about to put you into the most capable hands in town." I can hear her still shouting at me as I press the redirecting button. "Incoming," I say to Tony and press his extension. His telephone rings, and he answers it in his most placatory of voices.

Jesus Christ, I think, hanging up the phone somewhat exhausted by that exchange. Can things get any worse?

I stand, listening in on Tony's conversation. He is an amazingly talented bloke. His ability to calm down a situation, bring out the humor and make people relax is incredible. Within two minutes of talking to the cocktail-dress woman, I can hear him laughing with her, telling a few jokes and sharing a couple of indiscreet stories of other guests who were caught out even more by our dreadful dry-cleaning service. By the end of the conversation, the woman hangs up, actually feeling lucky.

"I don't know how you do it," I say, after he puts down the phone.

"Practice." Tony grins across the desk. "Anyway," he adds. "I'd better get a shift on—I've got to get some dresses sent over from Harrod's within the next half hour."

"You'd better get on."

"Yeah." He looks at his watch. "Not long for you, now."

"Can't wait." I smile. "My sofa and TV await."

The telephone rings, and I pick it up.

"Hello?" comes a very familiar voice.

"Oh hello, Ben." I'm glad to hear his voice. "Are you on your way in? We've had quite a day here, mate. Oh my God, you just missed a woman with a big black vibrator in her bag, and the Texan is here, handing out pink ones like it's going out of fashion." Ben says nothing. He doesn't even laugh. "Ben?" I repeat. "Are you there?" I hear a small, weak cough down the other end of the phone. My heart sinks; my shoulders sag. I know what's bloody coming.

"The thing is, mate," he starts. "I'm afraid I don't feel too hot." He coughs again, as if to reiterate his point. "It's the flu, you know. It's a bad one. There's a lot of it going around at the moment. I've spent all day in bed, mate, trying to fight it off, you know, trying to get into work, and I have to say, it has defeated me." He coughs again. This one is a little more dramatic. Ben's good at coughing, but then again, he is a thirty-a-day smoker so he does have an advantage. "I'm sorry, mate," he says. "I just don't think I can make it."

I am so angry I can hardly speak. "Right," I manage.

"Mate," he says. "I really am sorry. There is nothing I can do." He coughs again.

"Yeah, right."

"Honestly, mate, " he says, his voice suddenly all feeble. "It's terrible. I really hope you don't get it."

That little comment really is the last straw, and I'm afraid I lose it. "Why don't you piss off," I say suddenly.

"What?" he says.

"Piss off," I repeat. "You're always bloody doing this."

"Are you calling me a liar?" he says, sounding suitably outraged. He adds another cough for effect.

"I'm not calling you anything."

"Because, if you are, I will report you to Adrian . . . when I'm well enough to come in," he declares.

"Do what you want." I can hear him trying to answer back as I hang up the phone.

Well, things have now certainly become a whole lot worse. I lean on the desk, my forehead in my hands, working out the ramifications of Ben's sudden attack of the flu: a double shift, a bloody double shift. One of us is going to have to pull a double shift. And I know, for a sad, dismal fact, that it is going to be me. Shit. Liz has only just come off doing nights, so she'll make some boring song and dance about not doing it tonight. I may as well save myself the dull song and dance and volunteer to go straight through till 7:00 A.M.

Ben is so unreliable. As well as all his Housekeeping sex, and slacking on the job, Ben is a bit of a boozer. Perhaps, more accurately, Ben is an alcoholic. A drink problem is an occupational hazard in this business—Steve, Ben, there are a whole load of them. I'm not sure whether it's the pressure of work and the odd hours that are the contributing factors, or if boozers naturally gravitate to a place where the stuff is available twenty-four hours a day. Either way, Ben is an annoying little shit. This is the third time that he's pulled a sickie in the last month. He gets too drunk to come into work, and then calls up with some spurious excuse like his mother is ill, his boiler has broken, or he's got food poisoning; he's never that imaginative. Although, I have to say that tonight he didn't actually sound too pissed. Usually, he is slurring all over the place, and the fact that he has been drinking is so obvious, you actually don't want him to turn up for work.

I can't tell you how angry I am. I hate doing nights—there's nothing worse. It's not the staying up that bothers me. I've got a packet of Pro-Plus caffeine pills in the back office drawer to make sure I don't sleep on the job, plus I'm sure that Gino—stock check notwithstanding—will slip me a few vodkas later on, when things get desperate. It's just that nights are a nightmare. Between two and three in the morning, the hotel always goes a bit mad. Actually, it doesn't go mad, it goes totally in-fucking-sane, and I'm not sure if I'm in the mood to handle it tonight. All I want is a sofa and the telly. Instead, I've got Sodom, Gomorrah, and Bedlam rolled into one.

I don't know why it happens, exactly. All I know is that something strange occurs to a guest as soon as they check into the hotel. For some reason, even if, in real life, they are perfectly well-mannered, decent people with proper, balanced relationships, as soon as they spin though the revolving hotel doors, the normal rules of behavior no longer seem to apply. Their boundaries are altered; their rules of engagement change; they forget their responsibilities. And their inner diva or bastard child roars to the surface—they think they're invisible. They think that they can behave like rock stars on a bender, and then turn up at Reception the next day like innocent little children, butter hardly melting in their mouths. What they forget is that we're sober and we see and hear everything.

"You look a bit pissed off," says Liz, coming back from her macaroni supper.

"I'm furious," I say. "Ben's pulled a sickie."

"What? Again?"

"Yup."

"Are you sure he's not genuinely ill?"

"I can't believe you are actually asking me that," I say. "You know Ben as well as I do."

"Sorry," she says. "You're right."

"Yeah, well . . ."

"I can't do a double tonight," she says quickly. "I've got a date, and it's been planned for over a week. I really can't cancel it."

"No, don't worry. I'll do it."

"You will?" she says, sounding shocked.

"Yeah, well. You've got a date and everything. I'm only disappointing my sofa and I'm sure it will cope."

"Oh, thank you," she says, leaning forward to kiss me on the cheek. "You're a lifesaver."

Liz is all jolly and excited. Not only does she not have to do the night shift, but she is going out on a date. Looking at her again as she checks in some businessman, I see that she's redone all her makeup. Her hair is brushed, she's put more of that perfume on again, and she's put a dark maroon line around her mouth: she's definitely ready go out.

The Harrod's deliveryman arrives, much to Tony's delight, with an olive-and-gold box full of clothes. Jez is sent up to Room 404, and Tony earns himself another big fat tip.

Reception is beginning to fill up again. There are locals coming in for a postwork drink before winding their way home, and gaggles of glamorous girls meeting up for a bottle of champagne before going out to dinner, there are friends of guests of the hotel joining them for a drink before dinner, there are businessmen coming in for a networking drink, and there are the cord-clad dullards arriving for their pretheater dinner.

Pretheater dining is one of the most annoying things that a luxury hotel has to do. And it's not even that popular. We serve a light supper in the dining room that consists of something like a plate of smoked salmon, or a quiche and salad, or a bowl of soup, or an omelette stuffed with something, so that their stomachs don't rumble in the second half. It irritates the hell out of the kitchen, coming as it does in one of its busiest periods of the day just as everyone is running around like lunatics trying to get things ready for dinner, as well as sending out thousands of canapés into Banqueting. We try and knock out the theater food and get them in and out as quickly as possible, pretending that it has something to do with getting them there before curtain up. Which, of course, has nothing to do with it; it's just that we really don't want them cluttering up the dining room, before the real diners arrive.

Pretheater diners are always the most dull-looking people: petulant teenagers being forced on a cultural night out; middle-aged women with their middle-aged female friends; elderly couples. They are also never going to see anything interesting—it's usually *Les Misérables* or something else that has been going for decades. But the most annoying thing about pretheater diners is that they come back for pudding after the show. Just when you thought you wouldn't have to see them again, they turn up at about 10:45 P.M.—exactly when the kitchen is beginning to wind down after an exhausting night, and they demand a sticky toffee pudding to send them off to bed. Honestly, I've never really understood why we do it.

I ring through to Adrian's office to tell him of Ben's sudden and unexplained sickness, and I can tell that he is not impressed. Adrian used to be quite good mates with Ben, but recently he has begun to keep his distance. Adrian's an ambitious bloke, he hasn't gotten this far this quickly on talent alone; he's picked his friends carefully, he's been nice to the right people and he knows which clients to suck up to. Talking of which, I've just spotted Mrs. Dickson and her horrible yapping dog.

Steve's on her case, or should I say, cases, right away; he's got two in each hand as he comes through the revolving door. Mrs. Dickson manages to take care of her dog. She looks the other way, or is somehow totally immune to its barking and thrusting attempts at nipping other guests' ankles. Dressed head to toe in pink Chanel, she has hard yellow hair, a powdered white face, clumpy false eyelashes like dead spiders, and she bears more than a passing resemblance to Barbara Bush. Liz seamlessly makes an exit to the back room, leaving me to do the honors.

"Good evening, Mrs. Dickson," I say, impressing her with the personal touch.

"Is it?" she asks. "It may be for some. But I've had a terrible journey here."

"Oh really? I'm terribly sorry to hear that."

"Good," she says. "Now what suite do you have for me this time? I do hope it is better than the one I had last time. I can't remember which one it was. Sergeant!" she shouts down at her dog pulling on its lead, as it valiantly tries to have sex with Jez's leg. Poor Jez is not having much luck this afternoon. "Get off that man!" she continues. Sergeant continues to bark his annoying little lungs out.

"We have put you in Suite 560," I say with a full service-industry smile.

"560?" she asks. "Where is that?"

"Right at the top, with a view over the communal garden square."

"Communal?" she says. "I don't think I want to look down on anything communal."

"It is really very attractive," I say weakly.

"That's as may be," she replies. "But I think I prefer a more exclusive view."

While I try and convince Mrs. Dickson of the merits of her communal gardens view, wishing that I had simply said the word "gardens" and been done with it, Mr. Masterson wanders back down into Reception. His loud voice drowns out the chatter of people coming in for early evening drinks and Sergeant's shrill little bark. Jez and Dave stand to attention like soldiers on parade; it is an action that obviously pleases him, because he gives them both a fiver. But it is Tony he has come to see. He makes even louder than usual noises about his table at Sheekey's tonight. Slapping Tony on the back, he shakes his hand and gives him another note and then wanders back through to the glass doors in the direction of the bar.

"Good Lord," says Mrs. Dickson, her white nostrils curling

as if she has just smelt some frightful odor. "Who on earth is that?"

"Mr. Masterson." I add, totally unprofessionally: "He is a Texan oil millionaire."

"Oh," she says, like the source smell has been confirmed.

"He's a regular. He normally has your suite, 560, but as you have it this time, he can't."

"Really," she says. "Isn't that interesting, Sergeant?" she looks down on the floor, conversing with her dog. She picks a complimentary mint out of the bowl on the desk and throws it on the floor. Sergeant crunches and consumes it in a matter of seconds. "I think we'll take 560, after all."

I check Mrs. Dickson in, and she, plus Sergeant, get into the elevator while their luggage remains in the lobby. Dave and Jez practically draw straws to see who is going to have to take it up to her room. Like the French couple earlier this afternoon, Mrs. Dickson does not believe in tipping, or at least, certainly not in this hotel. Seeing as a small portion of it belongs to her husband, she thinks that all its staff and services come free. Jez loses yet again, and is dispatched with Mrs. Dickson's bags and what looks like Sergeant's dog basket. It really isn't his lucky day.

Liz comes back to the front desk and, while I'm not on my own, I decide to pop through to the bar to inform Gino that it is not my lucky night either, and I am being forced to pull a double. It's not because I want his sympathy; it's because I want his booze. Sometimes I pay for it, but more often than not, he gives me a freebie. He only really does it if I've got to go straight through. Although, the findings from today's stock check could change things.

The bar is heaving when I walk in: there is a real buzz in the place; all the tables are full and the ashtrays are getting that way too. There is so much noise that it's a wonder that anyone can hear the ebullient conversations they all appear to be having. There's a particularly loud group of young men in the far corner of the room drinking Dom Perignon Vintage 1995 champagne that retails at £172 a bottle. And there are a couple of glossy-looking girls at the bar, applauding Gino as he does the whole Tom Cruise thing with a cocktail shaker.

It's at times like this that Gino's real star quality shines through. He is the difference between a bar that is packed and earning its own space in revenue, and a moribund place full of miserable old men with flatulence.

Gino works the room. He serves the girls their cosmopolitan cocktails and tries to flog them his new "berrytini" creation—a martini made with blueberries. He then immediately makes sure that the boys on the other side of the room have enough champagne. At £172 a bottle, you can see why he is only too happy to help them consume just that bit more. He walks past Mr. Masterson and offers to light his £500 cigar, saluting as he walks back to the bar, another order for a £40 shot of twenty-year-old Talisker whiskey under his belt.

"Gino," I say, as I approach the bar.

"Hello there, mate." His eyes are shining with commercial delight.

"I just wanted to say that I'm doing a double shift tonight, so any problems in the bar, any hassle, you know where I am."

"Yeah, OK," he says, standing back from the till, letting Francesco cash up. "And any spare something to come your way?"

"Well." I smile.

"When that stocktaking fucker has gone." He nods towards the back.

"Is he still here?" I am surprised at Gino's frankness, with the man so close.

"Yeah, he is leaving in ten minutes." Gino shakes a fist in the general direction of the back room door. "I wish he'd fucking hurry up," he says loudly, cupping his hand around his mouth, directing his insult backstage. "He is cramping my bloody style."

"I heard that," says Mr. Kent, as he comes through the door with his clipboard.

"So sue me!" Gino shrugs. "I have a £40 shot of whiskey to serve. You want to watch me do it, in case I spill 25p worth on the side?"

"No, thank you," says Mr. Kent. "That's my finish for the day."

"Thank God for that!" says Gino dramatically.

"And may I say, you run a very good bar, Mr. Lauri."

"Finally, fuck, he gives me a *complimento*!" says Gino.

"Yes, well," says Mr. Kent.

"I did tell you, you will not find your Bombay Sapphire thief here. Try Housekeeping, Mr. Kent, Housekeeping!"

"Don't worry, Mr. Lauri, it's their turn next week."

"Oh," says Gino.

"Anyway, I wish you a good evening."

"Good evening."

"Yes, well," I say to Gino. "See you later."

"Absolutely, mate. And don't worry about anything."

"Oh OK," I smile. "Thanks."

I walk back into Reception, suddenly feeling not so bad.

By the time I get back to Reception, Liz has already got her coat on. She is puttering around between the front desk and the back office, humming with excitement at her impending departure.

"Oh, there you are." She smiles. It is amazing how going home can improve someone's mood. "Two cleaners have phoned in sick."

"What, already?"

"Yup," she says, stapling some paper together. "Oh, I got you these out of the office drawer." She hands me over a packet of Pro-Plus pills. "It doesn't look like there are that many left," she adds. "Half a packet. D'you think that might do the trick? Or do you want to send Jez out to get some more?"

"No," I say, taking four out of the packet. "I'm sure I'll manage."

"Are you sure you should be taking that many at once?"

"I don't see how else I'm going to get through tonight."

"Are you sure?" she asks, sounding concerned.

"Yeah, well." I knock them back.

"See you tomorrow," she says.

"Yeah. And you'll have a new girl, Michelle's replacement."

"Mm." She doesn't sound too keen. "I wonder what she'll be like."

"Attractive, I've heard," I say, just to wind her up.

"Oh, good." She smiles, looking ever-so-thrilled. "Have a good evening."

"Will do," I say.

"Night," she says, as she walks past Tony.

"Night," he replies.

Reception is beginning to take on the appearance of a railway terminus. There are people walking into the bar, people coming in for dinner, and guests leaving the hotel for meetings, meals, or drinks somewhere else. A couple of gents in cashmere coats with heavy leather briefcases are walking through on their way for a drink, while other groups of what look like fashion people keep turning up fashionably late for the cocktails-and-canapés-do in what could loosely be termed our ballroom. Well, it is a room big enough for a ball, and we do often host a couple in there in the run-up to Christmas. But in truth, it's a large room with some molding on the ceiling, some gold lamps on the wall, a grand piano, and a whole load of gilt catering chairs.

But it is popular and often booked, especially in the evenings; we hold about two or three events in there a week. It is catered by the same kitchen as the rest of the hotel, but the waiting staff are entirely different. They are made up of casuals, casuals who are even more casual than the staff who actually work in the hotel, which is saying something. They are paid minimum wage, get no tips, have no regular working pattern and can be called up to work anything from a six-day week to a no-day week at a moment's notice. As a result, the turnover is high, and it is the sort of job that only attracts foreign students, Australians on their break year, illegals, and first-generation immigrants with few language skills and little choice. The casuals are not really considered part of the rest of the hotel: they arrive and leave by a different, side entrance; they have one small room with a few chairs in which to change; they are not fed; and they have very little contact with the rest of the staff of the hotel. In fact, if I am being honest, I don't think I have ever spoken a single word to a single one of them.

Two thin girls walk up to Reception in stratospheric heels and transparent dresses.

"Hi," says the blond one, waving a stiff white card. "Can you tell us where the perfume launch is tonight?"

"Oh," I say. So that's what it is, I think. "Through the glass doors, turn left and it's at the end of the corridor."

"Thanks," says the darker-haired girl as they giggle and walk off through the doors.

Steve walks into Reception, stamping his cold, desensitized feet on the Indian carpet. He rubs his large gloved hands together and removes his top hat, rubbing the crown of his sweaty head.

"Well," he exhales. "That's me finished for another day."

"OK, then," says Tony, looking up from his desk. "Are you off, then?"

"Yup." Steve nods, wiping his running, defrosting nose on the back of his hand.

"Been a good one?"

"Good." Steve taps his jangling pocket. "And with that Yank up top, excellent," he says. "It's Dennis up next, isn't it?"

"That's right," says Tony. "Talking of the fat bastard, here he is."

"Alright? Alright? Alright?" says Dennis, as he walks up to Tony's desk, suited and booted and ready to go.

"Cutting it fine, Dennis. Cutting it fine," declares Tony, tapping his watch.

"Five minutes," says Dennis. "The traffic was shit."

"Yeah, right," says Tony. "You only live around the corner."

"Got me there," smiles Dennis, gloved hands in the air. "Caught me out." He turns around. "Alright there, mate?" he asks me, giving me an expansive wave across the room. "I thought I was on with Ben?"

"Alright there, Dennis," I say. "Ben's pulled a sickie, so I'm afraid you've got me tonight."

"You on a double?"

"Yeah." I nod, putting my hands together and bending my head to one side, making as if to go to sleep.

"You poor bastard. D'you know, Tony," he says, turning back around. "That wanker Ben wants sacking. Twice this week I caught him sleeping in the back office. He's a scumbag shit. . . . Don't worry, mate." Dennis turns back towards me. "I'll look after you. You stick with me."

"Alright," I say, smiling back.

I like Dennis: he is always a laugh to work with. Although he's Steve's cousin, he is actually nothing like him. He's more like Tony: he's handsome, he's got the gift of gab, and he is nearly always in top form. He also seems to like his job as doorman, he's been here long enough. But judging by the amount of time his cell phone goes off all the time, I'm sure Dennis has got a lot of fingers in a lot of other pies.

He stands around for a couple of minutes, sharing jokes with Tony and Steve, but a cab pulls up outside and he's out the door before you can say one-pound tip.

The telephone goes, and it's Lynette asking about check-ins. She sounds hassled and stressed, and then she finally admits that she has overbooked the hotel. This is the last thing I need on top of my hangover and my double shift. I hate having to turn people away who have booked into the hotel, because they normally go through the roof. It is understandable, I know, but it doesn't make it any more pleasant.

"We've got a couple of junior suites available," she says. "And that's it."

"Yup," I confirm, checking on the computer system.

"So you can upgrade the next few doubles who come in and after that, that's it," she says.

"How about using the large £2,500-a-night suite next to the Texan?"

"No," she says, swiftly. "Unless they are regular, regular, regular. But I can't see anyone who is."

"Right. And where are we sending them tonight?"

"The Berkeley."

We're always doing this, packing people off to The Berkeley. The Lanesborough sends their guests there and to the Four Seasons. The Savoy passes on to Claridge's, The Berkeley, or The Connaught. Claridge's passes on to The Dorchester, and The Dorchester to Claridge's. They do like to try and keep it in the group. The Sanderson uses St. Martin's Lane and The Metropolitan, and the two of them reciprocate. But only in the final option, when all else fails, will anyone bump guests to rival hotels.

"Oh," she says. "Just so you know—you need to add these two names to the blacklist."

"Right." I bring the list up on the computer.

Lynette gives me the names of two men who are currently doing the rounds at the moment. The police have forwarded their names to the various luxury hotels in the capital and they have given both physical descriptions and their modus operandi. Apparently, they ask for a showing around the hotel to get the layout of the place, and come back at a later date, charm a key card from a chambermaid, and rob the place. And it's the small hotels or the unmodernized ones that are most at risk. Unlike the newer hotels that nearly all have the swipe card system, the old-fashioned cut key makes it easier to break in. Hotels have to be very careful how they display these keys, as often it really is only a matter of getting behind the front desk to gain access.

It is from this time period onwards that we have to be very aware of who is coming in and out of the hotel, and keep an eye on security. It is usually at night that we start to make mistakes, especially if you're dog-tired like me. Although I do have to say that these pills are really beginning to kick in now; it's like someone's pinned back my eyelids with toothpicks and my heart is racing. Maybe I shouldn't have taken so many at once. But I was feeling so shit and so exhausted, I don't really see I had any choice.

As I lean forward on the front desk, riding the caffeine rush, a vision of warped femininity slowly comes towards me. An overly tall woman in large, high shoes, with suspiciously thick, uniformly colored hair and an awful lot of makeup, is checking in. I recognize him immediately. He is one of a few of our transvestite guests who come and stay for the weekend so they can enjoy the freedom of being allowed to dress as they want, without any hassle from their wives, partners, or even the staff. This tall brunette is a regular; he is also, somewhat confusingly, a regular with his wife. On the occasions that he comes here in his brown wig, we have to call him madam, and when he arrives with his wife, we obviously call him sir.

"Good evening, madam," I say. Out of the corner of my eye I can see Tony smirking slightly, but I ignore him.

"Good evening," he says, a surprisingly deep voice coming out of his lipsticked mouth.

"Ms. Austin," he says.

"Right, Ms. Austin. You're actually in luck. Due to the fact that the hotel is very full tonight, I shall be upgrading your room to a suite." He looks thrilled. His bright pink mouth smiles. "At no extra cost."

"Thank you," he says, like I have done him the nicest favor in the world. "Thank you very much."

"It's my pleasure," I say. And it is. It is always lovely to be appreciated for things that we do, particularly as most of the time we only ever really get grief. "Will you be wanting a table in the Restaurant tonight?" I ask. I can't remember if he is a room service transvestite or not.

"That would be wonderful," he says.

"Leave it to me. Do you need any help with your bags?"

"No, thank you." He picks up his small overnight bag. "There's no need to trouble anyone."

I take an imprint of his credit card, hand over the key to a junior suite, ask Tony to keep an eye on the desk and, as Ms. Austin takes the elevator to the fourth floor, I follow him, heading in the direction of the glass doors and into the dining room to secure him a table.

The dining room is not yet busy. In fact, it is empty except for a couple of tables of Americans, who for some reason, like to eat dinner at 7:30 P.M. The rest of the room is all set up and ready to go, exuding a tense emptiness, the calm before the storm. André, the Restaurant manager, walks in from the direction of the bar.

"Arrrgh," he says, shaking his small, white clenched fist. "That bloody Gino Lauri. I am so fed up with him."

"Why?" I ask, not really wanting to hear the reply, but I want a table from André at short notice, so it is better to hear his story.

"I go in to hand out some menus to some of the diners in his bar, and he throws me out of the place." Beads of angry sweat are glowing on his top lip.

"Well." I am somewhat stumped. "Um, that's not very nice."

"Not nice?" says André, turning to look at me like I'm some offensive little turd. "Not nice! It is more than not nice. It is war!"

Gino and André are always at odds, particularly at this time of night. The problem is that they want different things. André wants as many people in his restaurant as early as possible, so he can either get them out quickly, or so that he has more time to work on them, getting them to spend money on ludicrously expensive wines, like the £12,500 magnum of Chateau D'Yquem he managed to get James to buy him the other day. Meanwhile, Gino wants the guests to stay in his bar as long as possible so that he can try and sell them ludicrously expensive cocktails. The two of them are, quite simply, never going to agree. And they are also, quite simply, never going to be friends.

"Right," I say, not wanting to be drawn into Andre's war in any way, shape, or form. "Good luck." I smile.

"Yes, well," says André with a dramatic shrug. "What do you want?"

"A table."

"A table for what: one, two, three, forty?"

"One," I say.

"One." He sighs. "This is not a table-for-one restaurant. This is a destination restaurant and we don't do tables for one."

"They're a guest in the hotel," I insist.

"Oh, OK." He sighs, walking over to his large wooden lectern, he leafs through the oversize leather book that all the reservations are written in. "They can have Number Four," he says. "At 9:15 P.M. What's the name?"

"Austin."

"Austin," he repeats.

"Thank you," I say. "See you later."

Back in Reception, and Tony is flat-out, booking cabs, calling up restaurants to say that some guests are late, but assuring them that they are on their way. There are also a couple of rooms demanding to have shirts pressed and shoes polished, and Tony's sending Housekeeping to iron shirts, and telling guests who require shoe polishing to leave their shoes outside their bedroom doors in the appropriate bags provided and someone will deal with them before morning.

The telephone rings again. It's another of the night cleaners phoning in sick. It's another case of tactical food poisoning. I simply write down the name and ring downstairs to tell them they are three cleaners short so far tonight. There is no point in calling the cleaner's bluff: they get paid little enough as it is; if they want to lose a whole day's pay, it is up to them. But you would have thought that was the last thing they needed. Maybe they are genuinely ill, after all; there is always that possibility.

Mr. Masterson comes through the glass doors, not so fresh, from the bar. Not only does he look like he's had more than just a few of shots of Gino's overpriced whiskey, but he brings a cloud of Trinidad Diplomatic smoke along with him. The whole of Reception stands to attention as he arrives. Jez and Dave place expectant smiles on their jaded faces and Tony finishes his telephone call with brusque efficiency.

"Mr. Masterson," says Tony, getting out from behind his desk, tucking his tie into his trousers. "Your Mercedes is waiting for you outside."

"Good," says Mr. Masterson, pointing a red finger in Tony's direction. "Good man."

"I have instructed it to wait outside the Restaurant for you, sir, and bring you straight back here afterwards. But obviously, if you have any other plans, you only have to tell the driver and he will do exactly as you wish."

"Good," says Mr. Masterson. "Very good work." He walks up to Tony and taking two twenty-pound notes out of his wallet, he folds them, and pops them into Tony's top pocket, tapping them down with his finger. Tony smiles, but I know he hates it when people do that to him: it makes him feel cheap.

"Evening, sir," he says, as Mr. Masterson makes his way towards the door. "Have a good night."

"Thank you, Tony," Mr. Masterson touches the top of his head as he goes.

Dennis is at the Mercedes door like a shot. He tips his top hat, as Mr. Masterson lowers himself onto the cream leather seats, earning five pounds as he does so.

"Who the fuck does that man think I am?" mutters Tony, taking the money from his top pocket. "A fucking lap dancer?"

Speaking of which, I suddenly spot two suspicious women walking into the hotel Reception area. I don't know whether it is Tony's lap-dancing analogy, or the fact that both of them are wearing very short skirts and very high heels, that make me think that they might be prostitutes.

I know I said that we turn a blind eye to prostitutes, but only if they have been invited in by clients. If they are overt, by the hour, and soliciting in the hotel itself, then they have to go. And these two look very much like they are in the last category.

"Excuse me, ladies," I say, coming out from behind the desk, approaching them with confidence. "Can I help you at all?"

"No, thanks," says the taller of the two, in the shorter skirt.

That is not a good sign. "Are you sure?"

"Quite sure," says the other one.

They are standing in Reception, looking left and right like they have never been here, so they're clearly not guests. And, as they haven't asked for the bar, they are clearly not meeting guests either.

"Well, I'm terribly sorry, ladies," I say, with a light laugh and what I hope sounds like acres of charm. "If that's the case, I'm afraid I am going to have to ask you to leave."

"Leave!" squawks the tall one.

"We've only just got here," adds the second.

"Well, I'm terrible sorry," I say, walking towards the taller one with my arm out to guide her towards the front door. "We don't allow single women in here on their own."

"What?" says the tall one. "What are you talking about?"

"I'm afraid you won't find any clients in here, dear," I say, sort of spelling it out for her.

"Clients!" she exclaims. "What do you think I am? A prostitute?"

"Well . . ." I laugh.

"Gina!" she says. "Can you believe it? A prostitute? Jesus Christ! Get those invitations out, and get your hands off me," she demands.

"We've been invited to the perfume launch," says Gina, waving the invitations right close up to my face. "So you can piss off, you pervert," she says, looking me up and down. "Honestly," she scoffs.

"Wanker," says the taller girl, as they walk through the glass doors in the direction of the ballroom.

Tony is crying with laughter. He can't believe how badly I handled the whole situation. Perhaps it's because I'm so tired and run down, but I really can't believe that I did it, either. It's not really something that I am prone to doing, walking up to random women in Reception and accusing them of living off immoral earnings. But, in my defense, we do usually get a couple in during the course of an evening, willing to chance their luck in the bar, and it is my job, along with Tony or Dennis, to see that they don't make it in there.

Tony's putting his coat on and laughing at the same time. "I can't believe you, I can't believe you," he keeps on saying. "Nothing like prostitutes, the pair of them. Nothing like it." Even Jez and Dave are finding my fuck-up to their amusement, as they snigger, not quite so openly, into their coats.

It is the end of the shift for all three of them and, by the sound of things, they are planning a quick trip to the pub. It is Tony's idea, and Tony will pay for all their drinks. It is his way of building up a team and getting together a bit of loyalty; he's clever like that.

"Right," he says, rubbing his hands together. "Are we all ready for a swift one at the Rose & Crown?"

"Yes, please." Both Dave and Jez reply in unison, their tired faces momentarily lighting up.

"See you later then, mate," he says, waving to me. "Keep those eyes open for prostitutes," he sniggers. "You never know where you might find them."

"Yeah, right," I say. "You can all piss off."

"So can you." Tony smiles, pulling up the black velvet collar of his gray overcoat. "Has anyone seen that Paddy, Patrick, anywhere?" he asks, squinting as he looks outside.

"I'm here," says the diminutive voice of the equally diminutive Patrick.

"You're late," says Tony, turning around to find Patrick standing in his gray-and-gold uniform by the brass luggage trolley.

"I'm sorry," he says.

"You should be," says Tony, looking him up and down. "And get yourself to the gents and do something with your hair."

"Right away, sir," says Patrick.

"Stop calling me sir."

"Sorry, sir, sorry," says Patrick, shuffling towards the upstairs Ladies and Gents that is reserved for guests only.

"Not there," sighs Tony, clicking his fingers. "How many more times? The staff toilets."

He rolls his eyes, as Patrick jogs past him, his head down, on his way towards the back stairs. "See you later," he says to me, as all three of them head off to the pub.

Poor Patrick, I think, as the boy trots off down the stairs. Tony's only getting on his back because he is new. Patrick's been with us for three weeks, and all that time Tony's mercilessly taken the piss. He says it's for his own good. How else is the sixteen-year-old squirt ever going to learn? Who's going to show him the ropes or teach him the rules? But I suspect it's because Tony enjoys flexing his own power, you know, spreading it around a bit. Also, another thing is that Patrick was not Tony's first choice of bellboy/night porter; Patrick has the misfortune of being one of Adrian's appointments. So, as a result, Tony enjoys giving him plenty of grief. Poor sod; I swear the boy has developed a stammer and stress spots in the time that he's been here.

And I'm sure the lad is not really supposed to be on nights. He's been here such a short time, I have no idea how that can qualify him for the tricky job of night porter. He hardly makes me feel secure: the idea that I could leave Reception in his capable hands while I pop outside for a fag, or a quick slurp of vodka from the bar, is some sort of joke. I mean, he's fine when it comes to delivering faxes, collecting breakfast cards, and polishing shoes, but give him some aggressive customer, or some pissed-up group of men intent on trashing the place, and I bet you a whole ten pounds, you wouldn't see Patrick for dust.

There was an incident at the Covent Garden Hotel, where, apparently, two guys came into the hotel during the night, immediately went up in the elevator and quickly disappeared. The guys in Reception thought it was a little odd, and the night porter became a bit suspicious and said that he would keep an eye on the elevator and the stairs just in case. Anyway, one of the thieves got up and out onto the roof. He climbed into a guest's bedroom through an open window, helping himself to passports, handbags, and luggage before he left. They both then came running down the stairs and the night porter tackled one of them, hurling him to the ground. A huge fight then ensued, with the porter keeping one of the thieves pinned to the floor until the police arrived. They picked up the other villain a couple of days later.

Call me old-fashioned, but I don't really see nine-and-a-half-stone, sixteen-year-old Patrick pinning anyone, or indeed anything, to the floor until the police came. So, all I can say, in the grand scheme of all things violent is, thank God for Dennis.

"All right there, mate?" I say, as Dennis comes inside.

"Fine and dandy, me," says Dennis, sitting down at Tony's desk, putting his feet up. "You?" he says.

"Been better," I reply.

Dennis's cell phone goes off in his top pocket. "'Scuse me, mate." He pulls it out to answer it. He's not really supposed to be on his cell during work hours. It is supposed to be switched off, but Dennis is always breaking rules. He isn't really supposed to be sitting at Tony's desk either, especially when there's a leather padded chair provided for him. But who's going to tell on him? Certainly not me or Patrick.

Patrick comes back into Reception, his dark-red curly hair parted down one side and smoothed flat down on his head, like he is going out to Sunday lunch with his mother. I can't help smiling: he looks even younger than when he went down there.

"Alright there, Patrick?" I ask.

"Yes, thank you very much," he says, as he walks back to the brass luggage trolley and starts to rub it down.

The telephone rings on Reception. It's a woman on the second floor asking us to send someone up to zip her into her dress; she sounds terribly apologetic. I tell her not to worry, as we get these kinds of requests all the time; I've heard them all. One of the craziest I've heard was when Naomi Campbell was staying at the St. Martin's Lane hotel.

When extremely glamorous celebrities such as Naomi Campbell come to stay, they often are given one member of staff to look after them exclusively. In some hotels, you are given a butler, who will zip you into your dress or, on some more bizarre occasions, powder down your rubber catsuit for you. These people are often highly trained and are at the end of a beeper. They know how to tie a sari, they know in which order to place military medals, they can tie bowties, advise on white tie dress, coach guests on how to address ambassadors at receptions. They also know odd things like how to get the rarest of stains out of the frailest of fabrics.

Anyway a while back, before she cleaned up her act, Naomi had a member of staff who was on permanent call, to cater to her every whim. At around seven one night, she paged him, in a crisis, demanding that he come up to her room immediately. He arrived quickly, to find her sitting on her bedroom floor, clearly under the influence of a controlled substance, as she rocked back and forth, surrounded by piles and piles of makeup. She asked him to help find her lipstick. He wasn't quite sure what to do. He went into the bathroom and found lines of white powder racked up everywhere. He came out of the bathroom, picked up a random tube of lipstick from the floor and handed it over. It seemed to do the trick. He then made his very quick excuses and left.

But, I don't think the zipper-challenged woman on the second floor is going to be terribly difficult, so I send up Patrick. He needs to learn to cope with guests in all states of undress and all sorts of difficult and tricky situations, so he may as well be broken in as soon as possible.

He seems reluctant, and he is up and back in a flash. He must have spent all of fifteen seconds doing up the woman's dress. Yet, by the time he is back, polishing his trolley in Reception, the poor lad is so embarrassed that even the tops of his ears are pink.

Before I can tease him, Lynette comes through Reception in her coat. She is on her way home after a long day spent juggling rooms, guests, cancellations, and rebookings. She looks tired, and half of her eye makeup is slipping down her face, making her look like a panda.

"There you are," she says, sounding hassled. But then, I don't know of any time when she isn't. "Still here."

"Still here," I confirm. "Here all night. Ben is apparently terribly ill."

"Not again. He's always unwell, that boy." She stands at the front desk, distractedly shuffling through some faxes. "Now, right, there we are," she says, pulling out a piece of paper. "Right, Mr. Andrews. And Miss Cox."

"Yes."

"Well, the thing is, they have booked two adjoining rooms, if you see what I mean," she says.

"Right."

"And we don't have two rooms left, just a junior suite and a senior suite," she explains. "So I wonder if you can ask them to share."

"Share?"

"Yes, well," she says, looking slightly embarrassed. "They've been having an affair for six months at least, so I don't think they'll mind."

"Oh?"

"Well, they are both from the same company in Scotland, they come here often, they always take adjoining rooms; it doesn't take a genius to work it out," she announces. "And anyway, it always annoys me that they never use the other room, when we could easily resell it, which I suppose I have inadvertently done this time."

"Oh, right, of course," I say, feeling slightly stupid.

"Do you think that you can manage that?" she asks.

"I don't see why not."

"Offer them the suite, then suggest twin beds, and I guarantee you won't have any problems."

"Do you think it will work?"

"Well, in my years of experience, it has yet to fail. You have them on the back foot with the affair already; I don't think they'll want any trouble."

"OK."

"Anyone else you'll have to dump." She buttons herself up right to the top of her red coat. "Sorry," she says. "Good night."

"Night," I say.

"See you in the morning."

"I hope not."

"Of course." She smiles. "Sleep well, when you do finally get home."

She walks out into the night, and Mr. Andrews and Miss Cox arrive. And Lynette is proved right. It takes less than a minute of explaining and groveling and general obsequious behavior, before they accept the offer of the junior suite and decline the use of twin beds. You'd almost think that they wanted to sleep with each other right from the start.

With the furtive lovers dispatched to their junior suite, I say to Dennis that I am just going to pop downstairs for a cup of coffee and a cigarette to keep me going. He nods and mouths something along the lines of "OK." I'm not sure whether he means it for me, or for the person he is talking to on his cell phone. Anyway, I take my chance.

Downstairs smells of roast beef, disinfectant, and a faint whiff of truffle oil; it's hot and dark and relatively deserted, as I walk along the corridor towards the staff canteen. I serve myself a cup of black coffee and immediately take a sip. It's cold; not freezing, but cold enough to have an oily film on the surface. I drink it anyway—it's the caffeine that I'm after. Then I move on down the dark corridor to the smoking room, which I can smell a mile off. I sit down on one of the long benches beneath the line of blue nylon cleaning coats and light up. I sit, smoke, and listen to Chef shouting next door.

There's been a run on something: I can't quite make out what it is. It must be something warm and hearty; that always happens when it's raining outside, and tonight it's pissing down. It's amazing how we all order the same food when it comes to certain weather, and you can understand why some big food companies employ people to predict future rain or sunshine, because we all react like lemmings. I tell you, as soon as the sun comes out, we're all eating salads. A cold snap, or a downpour, and we are all ordering Chateaubriand, if we're lucky enough to be able to afford it.

I've seen it all before. The kitchen runs out of something delicious like roast lamb, Chef goes mad, getting pissed off with the predictability of his clients ordering the same thing, then eventually he tells a waiter he has no more lamb, the waiter then comes out and tells the restaurant manager, who eventually tells all the other waiters. In the meantime, three more orders for roast lamb have arrived in the kitchen, and some poor sod of a waiter has to go back out and tell the guests that they can't have their order. Nightmare, I think, as I take a long drag on my fag and thank God again I don't work down here anymore. Anyway, I think, a hotel of our standard shouldn't ever run out of anything.

I lean against the greasy wall in the smoking room and close my eyes for a second. There is no way I'm going to last the night, I think; even the pills aren't keeping me awake. I take another drag. Suddenly Patrick bursts through the door.

"There you are!" he says, all pink and sweaty and out of breath. "I've been paging you."

"It doesn't work down here," I say, taking the red pager out of my pocket. "There's no signal."

"Oh my God, you've got to come," he says, wringing his freckled hands with worry. "There's this Saudi guy upstairs and he's demanding a room; he says he comes here all the time and says that he wants a room right now. I don't know what to do. Dennis said to come and get you quick sharp, and I've been running around looking for you . . . everywhere," he adds, finally drawing breath.

Well, that certainly wakes me up. It's like having a rocket shoved up my arse and a big bag of Pro-Plus pills forced down my neck like a foie gras goose. I sprint fast as anything back up those stairs.

I come up the stairs, my heart racing, my hands sweating, to find a large Saudi dressed in his white robes and red-and-white-checked headdress waiting for me. Amazingly for a Saudi, his entourage is small, just two women, both dressed head to foot in black.

"Ah." He smiles as I approach. "The man we have been waiting for."

"I'm terribly sorry," I say, my chest heaving, as I arrive behind the desk. "It's just that we didn't expect you, sir."

"I know," he says with a wave of his hand. "I didn't expect to be here myself. Business is an unpredictable mistress, one is always at her beck and call."

"Right," I say, exhaling as I try and get my breath back. "I'm afraid to say that the hotel is very full tonight, sir."

"Oh. Is Adrian about?"

"The manager? Yes, of course, sir, um . . . yes, maybe, possibly, um, I'm afraid I don't know. I'll call for you," I add, like it is the best idea I've ever had.

"Good." His voice is quiet, yet extremely determined. He places his gold-ringed, manicured hands on the desk.

"Right," I say, nervously. "I'll call right away."

"Good," he says again.

I look up to see Patrick stumbling in through the doors with a heavy collection of expensive luggage under each armpit. Dennis comes through two seconds later carrying the same. They pile them high, one on top of the other, on the trolley. The Saudi turns around.

"There are three more in the trunk," he says.

"OK, sir," says Dennis, walking back out into the cold.

There is no answer in Angie's office, so I try Adrian's direct line, which is strictly, as he has reiterated many times before, for emergencies only.

"Hello," he says, sounding more than annoyed at being disturbed.

"You're still here," I say, the relief clearly audible in my voice.

"Of course, I'm still here," he says, like he never goes home to his girlfriend before 6:00 P.M. "I'm checking through the stocktaking."

"Oh, good."

"I'm glad you think it is good," says Adrian. "Anyway, what do you want?"

"I have a Mr. . . . ?"

"Sheikh—"

"I have Sheikh—here; he's just arrived, and he says he would like to see you."

"Jesus Christ!" says Adrian, coughing down the line. "Why the fuck didn't you say? Tell him I'm on my way."

"He's on his way," I say, with a wide service-industry smile, putting down the telephone. "He won't be a second."

"Good," says the Sheikh.

Indeed, Adrian is probably less than thirty seconds. I've never seen him make the distance between his office and here in such a short time.

"Sheikh!" he says coming through the glass doors, his silk tie flying in the wind. "How lovely to see you again. Really, it is lovely," he says. He stops, his hands outstretched now in a wide and welcoming manner. In fact, standing there like that, rooted to the spot, exuding ebullience, he looks a bit like Jesus.

The Sheikh is less forthcoming; he walks towards Adrian and offers his right hand to shake. "Good evening," he says. "How very pleasant to see you."

"Yes, wonderful," says Adrian, tugging on his hand like a one-armed bandit. "Excellent, excellent." He finally releases the Sheikh's hand, and comes around behind the front desk. "Right," he says, looking down the occupancy chart on the computer. "What do we have available for one of our old friends?"

Old friends—I almost snort; I've never clapped eyes on the bloke in my life. Although I do know that Sheikhs are obviously important people. He could possibly be the bloke who came in last summer when I was on vacation, and brought Michelle a pair of diamond earrings for being so special, and who also gave Tony a Cartier watch. Lord knows what he must have given Adrian for him to be that far up his Sheikhly arse, but it must have been something quite spectacular.

"Did you and your girlfriend enjoy your trip to Monte Carlo?" asks the Sheikh.

"Oh, very much so, very much so," says Adrian. "Terribly kind of you. Terribly kind, indeed."

So that was it, I nod. No wonder Adrian ran from his office.

It's just a shame then, for all concerned, that the Texan has the best suite in the hotel, so the Sheikh will have to make do with second best for the first time, I imagine, in quite a while.

"Oh, there we go," says Adrian, looking up, grinning from ear to ear. "How lucky, the best suite in the hotel is available tonight," he says. "Right at the top."

"The same as I had before." The Sheikh smiles, appearing satisfied.

"Ah." Adrian smiles. "Right, not quite the same room," he says. "It is the same but different. It is the same size, with two bedrooms, a lounge, two bathrooms, and another separate seating area, but it is slightly different."

"Oh?" says the Sheikh. "But the last time I came to stay, I had the best suite in the hotel."

"Yes," agrees Adrian, now rather regretting his initial boast. "We have two best suites."

"Interesting," says the Sheikh. "I had no idea that there could be two bests. One, I thought, had to be better than the other. But then again, my grasp of English never has been very good."

"Ha, ha, ha!" Adrian laughs somewhat hysterically, as he turns around to fetch the key. The Sheikh hands over his American Express Black card. "I'll just take a print of that," says Adrian. "And do you mind terribly, filling in this form? As we weren't expecting you, we haven't filled it in ahead of time." Adrian hands over a transparent plastic ballpoint pen. The Sheikh looks slightly repulsed. He bends down, picks up his briefcase, takes out a gold fountain pen, and proceeds to fill in the form.

Patrick is already waiting, the luggage stacked, ready to follow the Sheikh up in the elevator. Dennis, for some purely financial reason, is also in attendance. The Sheikh reaches back into his briefcase and pulls out two fifty-pound notes. He hands one to me, and the other to Adrian. "Thank you both for your help," he says. Patrick's eyes are round with astonishment; I feel mine doing the same. Adrian pockets his with professional speed and comes out from behind the desk, ushering Patrick, the Sheikh's two wives and the Sheikh on their way towards the elevator. As the door closes behind the party, Adrian visibly exhales.

"That was a fucking close shave," he says. "I'd hate to have bumped him to The Berkeley."

The cocktail party in the ballroom is coming to a close. Groups of inebriated guests are weaving their way through Reception on their way out to take a cab. With both Dennis and Patrick dealing with the Sheikh's copious amount of potentially very lucrative luggage, it is up to me to make sure the guests don't hang around in Reception too long, or start to make a nuisance of themselves. I can see a few groups peeling off into the bar. I know Gino won't mind too much, just so long as they are spending cash and not opting for cheap bottles of wine, instead of champagne.

A couple of drunken women sit down at Tony's desk and start pretending to use the telephone like it is the most original joke ever staged; little do they know that we have about six people a week doing the very same thing.

"Excuse me, ladies," I say, with a supposedly hilarious smile on my face. "Can you stop that, please?"

"Sorry," giggles one of them, as she gets out of the seat. The other laughs uproariously as they both totter out the door.

Some of our guests are beginning to come back into the hotel after dinner. A couple go back into the bar for some of Gino's expensive nightcaps and a couple more go upstairs to finish off the night in our Honor Bar on the fourth floor.

The Honor Bar is one of those new-fangled ideas that tend to be found in the smaller, cozier hotels. Our Honor Bar is new, just over a year old, and is one of Adrian's more revolutionary ideas. You either love or hate it. And Gino, somewhat unsurprisingly, hates it. He finds the idea that hotel guests would want a small, intimate bar, without a barman, insulting to say the least. Needless to say it also deprives him of customers. To be honest, the sort of people who tend to use the Honor Bar are the sort of people who would perhaps not sit downstairs, shelling out seventy-five pounds a shot for a glass of whiskey. And they usually fancy a quieter time than the hectic bonhomie of Gino's.

One thing is certain, people are pretty dishonorable when it comes to honor bars. Most of the time they will fail to write something down—their mixers, their nuts, their third vodka. They will sometimes deliberately write down a cheaper brand of wine, while serving themselves something expensive. Sometimes, it is not even intentional: they get too plastered to remember their room number, or exactly how many drinks they actually have had. Gino does occasionally send a member of the bar staff to check up on things. Either Gianfranco or Francesco pop up and down a couple of times during the night to make sure everything is running smoothly, and that no one has passed out on the sofa. But it is not a popular errand, as time out of the bar means time away from tips.

Ironically, the Honor Bar also doesn't make the hotel very much money. With all the thieving and alcohol-induced absent-mindedness that goes on, the place would run at a loss, if it weren't for the fact that we add a bit extra on the price of the drinks to compensate. The hotel would never want to be out of pocket, now, would it?

But with all the theft, drink price compensation, and covert supervising, it's a wonder a hotel bothers to have an honor bar at all. Rather like Jacuzzis in the suites, and large heads on the showers, an honor bar is one of those modern things that a supposedly modern hotel can no longer do without. It indicates that you are stuck in the dark ages if you don't have one. It is also a nod to the new cosmopolitan traveler who expects his hotel to be a home away from home; where his every whim and creature comfort is catered to, including a couple of free vodkas, if he needs it.

Mr. Austin comes through Reception in a long print skirt and pastel shirt, on his way to dinner in the dining room. Both Dennis and Patrick wish him a good evening, as they all come out of the elevator at the same time. The two of them are smiling— pound signs light up their eyes.

"Fifty quid." Dennis smiles as he walks past, on his way to Tony's desk. "That's a nice little earner early in the evening."

"I know," says Patrick, smiling, his pale face sporting big pink excited patches. "It can't get any better than that."

"Oh, it can, mate," says Dennis. "Stick around, and there's a whole lot more where that came from."

I find myself feeling my fifty-pound note in my back pocket, thinking perhaps it was worth pulling a double shift after all.

Tony comes through Reception, talking on his cell phone, his navy cashmere overcoat flapping open as he goes. He doesn't pause to speak to any of us; he only dishes out a small businesslike wave. As he walks out of the revolving doors, another young man comes in. He makes his way up to the front desk.

"Room 220," he says.

"220," I repeat, as I tap in the room number. The room is occupied. "Is your wife or partner in the room before you, sir?" I look up.

"No," he says. "I'm on my own. Is there some sort of problem?"

"Um, well, I'm not sure, sir. Could you tell me your name, and I'll just check on the computer?"

"Mr. Grey," he says. "My name is Mr. Grey."

"Right." I have to say, I'm beginning to sweat a bit. Either I've got a sixth sense that something is wrong, or I've had way too much caffeine. Both are very possible. "Mr. Grey you say." I look down and see that the room has been sold to Mr. McGrath. Fuck. Fuck. Fuck. My heart is now beating really rather fast. My palms slip with sweat. This is the bastard whose room I packed up at lunchtime this morning. Jesus Christ, I don't believe it. I'm going to kill Ben when I see him. Why do I have to be on a double? "Ah," I say.

"Is there a problem?" he says, leaping down my throat at the earliest opportunity. "It's the same room I've been in for the past three days."

"Yes," I say. "The room you were supposed to check out of this morning."

"No I wasn't," he says, quickly and aggressively.

"Well, according to our records, you were."

"Your records are wrong."

"Yes, well, in your absence, sir, they are all we can go on."

"What is that supposed to mean?"

"What it means, sir, is—"

"Actually, I don't care what it means," he says, slamming his fist down on the desk. Dennis, still on his cell, gets out of his chair on the other side of Reception. "I demand to go to my room."

"But that's just it," I say, trying to sound as nonconfrontational as possible. "It is no longer your room. It is occupied by someone else."

"What?!" he says, taking a step back, like I've thrown a glass of cold water in his face. "What do you mean, someone else is in there?"

"Well, I'm afraid we checked you out," I say calmly.

"You did bloody what?"

"There's no need to swear, sir."

"What do you say?" he says, leaning towards the desk, fury flushing across his face.

Shit. Fuck. No, I should not have said that. I'm the person in the wrong here, and I am not handling the situation with any great aplomb.

"I'm terribly sorry, sir," I say. "I'm afraid that we have sold your room to someone else, as we believed you to be leaving us today."

"Fine, right," he says, trying to get a grip on what I am saying. "So give me another room."

"Ah." I can see him bristle. "There aren't any other rooms."

"What?" He is now looking so angry, I can't get eye contact with him. "I want to see the manager."

"He's just left for the evening," I say.

"What!!" He is almost screaming. "What sort of fucking place are you running here?"

I'm tempted to say the word "hotel" but decide against it, as I sense it might send him through the roof. "I'm terribly sorry, sir," I say again. "I could get you the duty manager, but there is nothing I can do. We have obviously made a terrible mistake here, and sadly there is nothing I can do to rectify it." Mr. Grey just stands there dumbfounded. "We can arrange for you to stay free of charge at The Berkeley tonight, on the hotel, and we will obviously compliment your next stay with us."

"If you think, for one fucking minute, that I am ever going to stay here again, you have another fucking think coming," he says, his eyes becoming bloodshot.

"I understand perfectly, sir." I turn around and go into the back office and return with his packed suitcase.

"You've packed my bags?" he whispers.

"Yes, sir," I say, half closing my eyes, waiting for the outburst.

"You lot are un-fucking-believable. Call yourself a five-star hotel?" he yells, leaning over the desk. "Call yourself a fucking luxury establishment? You wouldn't know the meaning of service, if it fucking came along and ripped your fucking head off."

"Yes, sir," I say.

He bends down and picks up his bag. He marches towards the revolving doors.

"Excuse me, sir," says Dennis. "I've arranged for a complimentary cab to take you to The Berkeley."

Mr. Grey stops in his tracks, and turns to Dennis. "You can FUCK OFF as well!" he shouts, at the top of his voice.

"Yes, sir," says Dennis. "Have a good evening, sir."

Mr. Grey scrabbles through the revolving doors, which he tries unsuccessfully to slam in his fury.

"That went well," says Dennis, with a wink.

"Yup," I say, exhaling loudly, trying to force out some tension. "I think I've just cost the hotel over a thousand pounds."

"And the rest," says Dennis. "I don't imagine for one second he's going to hold back when it comes to his minibar tonight."

"No," I agree. "And I also can't imagine us trying to get any money out of him, either."

"Don't think so," says Dennis.

"Shit."

"You can say that again."

"I'd better ring The Berkeley and warn them he is coming."

"That would be a nice thing to do." Dennis smiles. "Rather them than me."

While I'm speaking to the guy on the front desk at The Berkeley, explaining to him all that has happened, I see Mr. Masterson come back into the hotel. His face is all red and jovial and relaxed, he has obviously had a fine dinner at Sheekey's. He makes his way over to Dennis and sits on the corner of his desk and starts to have a chat, which I try and listen to with one ear, while hearing the chap at The Berkeley with the other. Sadly, such multitasking is beyond me.

After I put down the phone, I wait for Mr. Masterson to disappear into the bar and the grateful arms of Gino, before asking Dennis what his conversation was all about.

"He was asking for an 'extra pillow,'" says Dennis.

"Oh lord," I say, looking at my watch. "It can't be that time already."

Dennis is quite capable of getting guests "extra pillows" if he wants to, needs to, or has to; but it is not something that he particularly advertises. He has a couple of numbers for discreet ladies of the night up his sleeve, but they are only for the most valued of customers. If anyone other than Mr. Masterson asked Dennis for a prostitute, he would look down his rather short, turned-up nose, and pretend not to understand. Even if he does get a backhander for doing so. But, seeing as it is Mr. Masterson, he gets on it right away.

I hate to be the one to say it, but, for a supposedly God-fearing, puritanical nation, Americans love their whores. I'm not sure whether it is because they usually have lots of money, and are far away from home, but it's true. Mr. Masterson's request on his way back to the bar was as inevitable as his splashing on ridiculously expensive whiskey. The Japanese are the same: they love their whiskey and their whores just as much as the Americans.

Although, it is normally the more mature guest who pays for sex. These days, the young guys aren't so keen. It is usually the fiftysomething bloke who has his wife and kids at home who goes whore-mad in a hotel. He tends to be fat, he smokes a cigar, he's got the company credit card and he's going to really spend some cash.

Among the Europeans, it is the Germans who are the most keen on prostitutes. The French and the Italians aren't usually that interested, or maybe they just don't have the cash. And the Russians, bizarrely, usually bring their own. They either travel with them, arriving in the hotel with a couple of girls at one time, or they somehow always manage to come back to the hotel in the evening with a Natasha in tow.

The English, on the other hand, seem to prefer gay sex. I know it sounds odd, but whenever they get a bit pissed in the bar, they start coming on to the staff. We have a couple of regular guests who stay here who are quite keen on their rent boys; but so long as it's kept quiet and no one is obvious about what they are doing, we turn a blind eye. What you get up to in your own room is your own business, particularly if you are shelling out two grand a night.

I'm pretty sure Dennis can get you drugs as well. Not smack, but a couple of grams of charlie, speed, or a few E's have most certainly slipped through his fingers of an evening, but only if you are rich enough, you spend plenty of it in the hotel, and you tip him handsomely afterwards. That's the thing about those little extras in the concierge service, you have to be the right person, asking in the right way, otherwise, I'm afraid, you'll get absolutely nothing. And nowhere more than in the luxury hotel business do double standards apply.

Dennis is muttering and sourcing "extra pillows" on the telephone. He occasionally laughs heartily at some shared joke. The Reception area is busy with guests and their friends coming back and forth, to and from the bar. But nowhere is busier at the moment than the Restaurant. This is a silly time, when well-lubricated guests are going to spend silly money on silly drinks.

I remember one such fabulous moment when Lord of the Dance, Michael Flattley, shelled out £3,500 for a bottle of Chateau d'Yquem 1921 dessert wine to impress a very trim, large-breasted blonde. The sommelier was doing star jumps in the kitchen, he was so thrilled that he'd finally managed to get rid of the stuff. I think it had been sitting in his cellar for over a year. After he'd served the wine, a couple of us minced past just to take a look, to see if they were enjoying it. I don't know how one is supposed to look when drinking more than a week's salary in a sip, but, as far as I was concerned, they didn't look ecstatic enough. They went on to leave half the bottle unfinished at the table; they must have had more interesting things on their mind. You should have seen the race to clear the table afterwards; we all helped ourselves to a slurp of the stuff. And I tell you, it slipped down like ambrosia.

But that is the thing with all these very expensive drinks, you wonder if they are actually worth it. These 1800 brandies that we have in the cellar go for more than £700 a shot, but half the time I wonder if they are actually what they say they are. I have no idea how anyone can tell if they are legit or not. I'm sure we've bought some dodgy stuff in the past and served it up to the customer all the same. Sometimes, guests order these expensive wines and decide, once they open them up, that they don't like them. It can be rather embarrassing. The sommelier has to stand there and tell them that the £1,500 bottle of wine they've ordered is not corked, it's just they are either too drunk, or simply don't have the taste buds to appreciate it. The sommelier doesn't say that, of course, but I have lost count of the times I have seen flushed, middle-aged men stand, swaying on the spot, while they demand a second opinion.

It is also more than the cellar man's job is worth to let any of this expensive stuff go off, turn, or cork. The equivalent of the national debt of a small country is kept in wine in our cellars and every single one of the bottles has to be turned, loved, and nurtured. No one can afford to have one £5,000 bottle of wine go to waste. It is a huge responsibility.

A middle-aged couple weave their way through Reception, pretending not to be drunk. Her skinny stilettos keep slipping on the shiny marble floor, while he keeps a firm grip around her waist, trying to keep her perpendicular. She appears plastered enough to nod when passing a pot palm, thinking it some animated object. They look like they've had a good evening.

My night has only really just started, I think, as I stare outside through the revolving doors, watching a taxi pull up outside and its door open. Patrick stirs to make the effort to open the door of the hotel, and my heart sinks like a stone. Walking towards me, an expectant smile on his face, is a small Japanese businessman. My head falls into my hands as I force myself to stand up. Oh God, here we go.

"Good evening, sir," I start. The poor man bows. Little does he know that in three minutes time I'm going to bump him, and he is going right back in a cab and off up the road to The Berkeley. Straight off his sixteen-hour flight, he still thinks we have a room for him. I, of course, know better. He pointlessly hands his bags over to Patrick who puts them on the brass trolley, and he gets out his passport. My toes are curling. The man looks exhausted. I go through the motions, pretending to look at Mr. Yammamoto's passport, typing his name into the computer, and then I come up with the usual bumping excuse.

"Oh," I say, pretending to be shocked. "Oh, dear." They always begin to look concerned at this point. "Oh, I am so terribly sorry, sir. It looks like there has been a mistake. We've had some terrible maintenance problems in the hotel today, and I'm afraid that your room is no longer available."

It is always important to pretend to the guest that there was a room available at the time of booking, and that a new, unavoidable problem has just surfaced which prevents them from taking the room. In short, it is an uncontrollable act of God that is forcing us to turn them away, rather than Lynette in Reservations overbooking the place again.

Mr. Yammamoto bows again, and takes the rejection in his stride. I tell him there is a place available for him at The Berkeley, and he thanks me for all my help. Patrick takes his bags back outside for him, Dennis hails him a cab and I ring The Berkeley to tell them there is another one on their way. That's sixty pounds I've earned so far tonight. For every new guest I send there, the management gives me twenty pounds; Tony would be proud of me.

But I do have to say that I feel sorry for the bloke. All that time in the air, only to touch down and find there is no room at the inn. Then again, it is always the single Japanese businessman who gets bumped. Lynette does it on purpose. As soon as she knows she's overbooked, she goes down the list to work out whom she can upgrade and whom she can bump. If, when you book your hotel room, you say it is some sort of special occasion, then you are more likely to be moved into a junior suite. If you book through a travel agent, the result is the same; it is a way of keeping the company sweet and the hotel in their good books. However, the lone traveler, here for one night, is always the first to go—hence the Japanese businessman. Repeat customers are usually accommodated in some way, and a multi-night booking is something to be looked after. The last thing you want to do is lose the hotel money, or affect its yield. So, time and again, in fact, every time, it's the Japanese businessman that gets it.

"Good night, sir," says Dennis, giving the bloke a little wave. "Have a good evening." His cell phone goes off again. He answers it, all jovial and upbeat. The call is short. "Shit," he says, as he hangs up. It looks as though "extra pillows" are hard to find tonight.

The telephone goes, on the front desk. It's some drunk calling down from his room, complaining about Room Service. Apparently the club sandwich he ordered over an hour ago is nowhere to be seen, and he can't raise them downstairs in the kitchen. I feel like telling the bloke that I'm not surprised. The kitchen staff are now reaching the absolute ends of their tethers, they have done something like 2,000 covers today, including breakfasts, early breakfasts, lunches, pretheater dinners, teas, snacks, a selection of canapés for four hundred, eats for the bar, and the last thing they want to make is some sodding club sandwich for a pisshead who will only eat half of it, before falling asleep fully clothed on his bed. But I inform the drunk that I'll go and investigate.

Walking into the kitchen is like going into the Amazonian rainforest: it is so hot and full of steam, my shirt immediately sticks to my chest. Despite the fact that things are beginning to wind down at the end of the day, the atmosphere is no less tense and frenetic. Chef is still shouting out last orders, leaning on some exhausted commis chef who is in the shit with his sauces. Meanwhile, some peppered beef is sitting on a plate under a heat lamp, slowly giving up the ghost. The same could be said for the staff: their shiny white faces have a haunted look to them. Under the unforgiving blue strip lighting, the large bags under their eyes look red and raw. They all look colorless, like animals that live under stones and rarely see the light of day, which is actually the case.

The small, dark-haired kitchen porter, who still doesn't speak much English despite working here for five years, is mopping down the floors with some stinking disinfectant. The chefs are working around him, walking blood and vegetable peelings back through his supposedly clean floor. A couple of men in whites are bleaching the sideboards where they make the starters, there are two more splashing down the food storage area and one man going at the stockpots. These are two enormous round barrels that stand side by side, containing carrots, onions, bay leaves, fennel, and chicken or beef stock; they are emptied, cleaned, washed, and scrubbed every couple of days, and the stocks are then made freshly again from scratch.

The noise is so loud that it is hard to hear oneself shout, let alone think. The crashing of metal against metal, the sound of the high-pressure water sprays cleaning out pans, and Chef's endless barking commands, all make it impossible for me to ask anyone where the hell the Room Service bloke is. The small room next to the kitchen where they take the orders is empty, and he is nowhere to be seen. Finally, I tap the kitchen porter on the shoulder and he turns around.

"Room Service?" I shout, very close to his ear. He doesn't bother to reply. But he makes a simple smoking gesture with his hand, and I understand what he means.

I walk back down the long, dark corridor into the smoking room and find two people in there. The first looks like one of the night cleaners who has turned up early for his shift. He is sitting there, in his green smock, smoking a cigarette and reading an Arabic newspaper.

"Good evening," I say to him. He looks so shocked that I have actually spoken to him that he doesn't say anything in reply. He nods the most imperceptible of acknowledgments and gets back to reading his newspaper. Curled up next to him on the bench and very obviously fast asleep, is the bloke who is supposed to be doing room service. He looks so happy there that I am loath to disturb him. Gently snoring, a quiet smile on his face, it is probably the happiest he has been all day. I bet the drunk has forgotten about his club sandwich by now. But then, he may not have, and it will be only a matter of time before he is down in Reception irritating the hell out of me. So I shake the Room Service bloke gently on his shoulder. He smiles, turns onto his back and stretches full length on the bench, like he has forgotten where he is. He opens his eyes and sits bolt upright with the shock of having me stare down on him.

"Shit, fuck, sorry," he says. He sounds French. He looks younger sitting up than he did lying down. I'd guess he is about twenty.

"Um, Room Service?" I say, more as a suggestion than a question.

"I know, sorry."

"Club sandwich."

"Fuck," he replies, and slaps his forehead. He is off the bench and out of the room before I can say anything else. I follow him out of the room, only to catch a glimpse of him running down the corridor to the kitchen.

"Good evening," I say to the night cleaner as I go to shut the door behind me.

"Good evening," he very tentatively replies.

Back upstairs, and Reception is still busy. Hopefully Dennis, in my absence, has been keeping an eye on who is coming in and using the hotel bar.

As regular closing time approaches, we often get a rush of late-night drinkers making their way in here. Licensing laws mean that if you are a guest in the hotel you are entitled to drink all night. But to be honest, it depends on what you are drinking, or if Gino can be bothered to keep the place open for you. People who aren't guests in the hotel are supposed to be gotten rid of before 11:30 P.M. although often, if they are behaving themselves and spending enough, we allow them to stay on drinking. I remember that in some of the places like The Halcyon hotel in Holland Park, in the more tucked-away bars, they stay open much later than anywhere more centrally located. That place was hidden from the police, and because it was in a basement, residents both in and outside the hotel were never disturbed. It used to stay open regularly till dawn.

There are also those more determined drinkers who get around the residency law, by booking themselves into a room that they have no intention of using, just to carry on boozing. These are the sorts of guests who make my day, so to speak, as I can charge them for a room that I know won't have to be cleaned and then I can sell it on to an early arrival first thing in the morning. Sadly, the hotel is full, so there'll be no booze bookings tonight.

Dennis looks like he's in a bit of a mood, as I walk over to check that everything is OK. I spot Patrick going to use the guests' toilet again. I can't be bothered to tell him off, and I don't really care if a guest spots him in there at this time of night; I don't think it matters. Dennis tells me that the hotel bar is pretty full already, with guests left over from the cocktail party in the ballroom. He suggests we could be in for a tough night.

"How's your search for 'extra pillows' going?" I ask, trying to tease him.

"Don't ask," he says, devoid of humor. "I had two women supposed to turn up half an hour ago. They're late."

"Two. Our Texan friend is greedy."

"I don't think he'll have both of them, it's just to give the man a bit of a choice."

"How thoughtful."

"There's no need to be sarcastic," he says.

"I wasn't," I say.

"Whatever," says Dennis.

"Oh my God!" says Patrick, running towards us, his already pale face turned totally white. "You'd better come with me," he says to me, beckoning urgently. "And Dennis, I think we should call an ambulance."

Patrick directs me into the downstairs Gents' toilets. Walking into the urinals, it looks like a murder has taken place. There is blood everywhere: pools of it shine on the white-tiled floor, splatters of it flick up the walls in lines and streaks, great gobs of it slide down the sides of one of the basins. And, in the middle of it all, lies a young man in a pin-striped suit, with his trousers down by his ankles, his penis hanging out and his two front teeth missing.

At first both Patrick and I think that he's dead, but it soon becomes apparent, through some incomprehensible mumblings, that he is still with us. Having ascertained, much to my relief, that he is still alive, I'm not sure whether to move him or not. There is something deeply undignified about his lying there with his penis out, but I don't want to damage anything. You always hear that you're not supposed to move injured people, but to leave him like this somehow doesn't seem right.

"Patrick," I say, as we stand there staring lamely. "Go and get a blanket from Housekeeping. I do think that we should cover the guy up a bit."

"Yes, right, right away," he stammers, glad to be given something to do.

"The ambulance crew are on their way," announces Dennis as he rushes into the Gents. "Jesus Christ," he says, stopping abruptly. He retches into his hands. "Oh my God," he says. "I fucking can't stand the sight of blood. Oh Jesus," he says, fanning himself. "The bloke's lips have gone fucking blue." I look down and sure enough, it looks like he's passed out and his lips are turning turquoise.

"Jesus Christ," I say, leaning over him. "We're going to have to give him mouth-to-mouth."

"Fuck off," says Dennis. "I'm getting out of here before I throw up everywhere." For a supposedly hard man, Dennis doesn't appear to have an iron gut. "I'll wait outside for the ambulance crew and tell them where to go," he announces, slamming the door behind him.

I bend down in the pool of blood, and cover his mashed-up mouth with my hand. I desperately try to remember the first aid course the hotel made us take about six months ago, where I sat at the back making paper balls out of my notes. I cover his nose with my mouth and start to blow. I look at his chest: it seems to be moving. I do the same thing all over again and wonder whether I should be pounding or massaging his heart. I blow again. He coughs slightly, his lips are looking a whole lot less blue. The ambulance crew bursts through the urinal doors. Dressed in their green jumpsuits and black boots, one of them says something along the lines of "we'll take over from here."

I walk out of the toilets in a daze; that was a bit of a close call.

I've no idea whether I did the right thing, or if I'd just performed something that was wholly unnecessary. A small crowd has gathered in Reception; there is nothing like a drama to gather a group of gawking drunks.

"All right, all right," says Dennis, having suddenly regained control over his emotions. "Move along now. Move along. There is nothing to see." He slowly moves a group carrying vodka-and-tonics and a few flutes of champagne back in the direction of the bar.

It's not long before the ambulance crew bring the young man through Reception, tucked under a red blanket. He is now clearly conscious, muttering madness as they take him out.

"Is he OK?" I ask one of the paramedics walking behind the stretcher.

"Oh yeah," he replies, with a seen-it-all-before sort of smile. "Turns out he slipped in the urinal while taking a piss, knocking himself and his two front teeth out."

"Oh right," I say.

"He was lucky you came along when you did. You gave mouth-to-mouth, didn't you?"

"Well, a couple of blasts."

"Things could have been a whole lot worse," he says. "He's lucky he's so pissed. He's going to feel it a whole lot more in the morning."

"Right," I say.

"You should clean yourself up a bit," says the medic, pointing down to my trousers, that are covered in sticky patches of blood. "That can't be a good look for the hotel." He smiles and pats me on the back, before walking out of the door.

Jesus Christ, I think I need a cigarette. I can't be bothered to go downstairs to the smoking room, so I wander outside. At this late stage of the evening, I don't think anyone is going to mind a few cigarette butts on the pavement. While I stand, leaning against a pillar outside the hotel, a couple of coppers pull up outside in a patrol car. I suppose they are obliged to follow up any ambulance call, especially if it is a luxury hotel. The police and the ambulance crew mix outside the hotel; I presume they are being told that no foul play is suspected. One guy looks like he is smiling: I suppose it is not every day you're told that a customer is so pissed that he slips and brains himself on a urinal. I think if they'd actually seen him lying in a pool of his own blood, they might find it less amusing.

I stub out my cigarette on the pavement and, as I look up, I clock Dennis's two "extra pillows" slipping into the hotel behind the police. They are easy to spot: long legs, long hair, short skirts—girls that obviously attractive are rarely seen unescorted, unless they're on the game.

I try to follow them into Reception, but they are so quick off the mark that, by the time I've made it through the police presence, it appears that the girls are already in the bar.

Dennis is already on his cell, recounting his passed-out-punter-with-his-cock-out story to his cousin at The Dorchester. He tells it well: ten minutes in the gestation and it already sounds like one of those unbelievable stories that he specializes in. I can hear his cousin laughing down the phone as I go past.

I go down into the bowels of the hotel in search of some new trousers. I know there is some cupboard, somewhere, where they keep a supply of black suit trousers because they form the bottom of the waiter uniforms.

It's very dark down here. I walk past the smoking room, the kitchens, and the staff dining rooms. I am in unfamiliar territory now; the hotel opens up like a rabbit warren of corridors and small rooms, all badly lit, with flickering strip lights and stinking of chlorine, cabbage, and stale cigarettes. The smell is so sweet and high it makes you gag if you breathe in too deeply. So I don't. I keep my hand over my mouth, and I walk along, occasionally opening cupboards to see what it's inside them. I come to a corridor of dining room linen, tablecloths and napkins piled high; some are plain white, others have those old-fashioned pastel borders on them that I haven't seen for a few years. Further along the corridor are shelves of cleaning equipment, bottles of bleach, yellow plastic containers of cleaning fluid, mops, buckets, and packet after packet of bright pink rubber gloves. Eventually, I come across one of the night cleaners collecting supplies.

"Evening," I say. The whites of his eyes blink at me in the dark. "Do you know where I can find any trousers?" I ask. The man does not reply. He blinks at me again. "Trousers?' I repeat, scanning his face for some sort of reaction. The bloke obviously doesn't speak any English.

A hotel cleaning job is the refugee's, or illegal immigrant's, first port of call. Hotels are notorious for employing people while looking the other way when it comes to documentation: they turn a blind eye to doctored passports; they happily employ cleaners with temporary National Insurance numbers. When you apply for a National Insurance number in the UK, you are give a temporary number which starts with "TN" followed by your date of birth, while Immigration looks into your eligibility to work. Most hotel workers have "TN" numbers and they have been working with them for years. If you have a "TN" number, you are charged an emergency tax rate, but when you are paid minimum wage, it barely makes any difference, as the amount is so small.

It is completely unsupervised. Hotels pay directly into workers' bank accounts, and see nothing wrong in sending someone's wages into an account under a totally different name. There have been cases of the Home Office storming into hotels, on an illegals' raid, to find out that over half the staff shouldn't be working there, and the names they are using bear no relation at all to what they're called. They then cart off thirty or so people and deport the lot of them. But then again, you can't really blame the hotels for trying: just so long as people have two hands to clean with, who gives a shit where they are from? There is hardly a queue of people around the block desperate to work those hours, in those conditions, for that amount of money.

Hotels are also good places for people to disappear into. Once we had this Colombian chambermaid who had a temporary Social Security number and a student visa. Technically, she was only allowed to work twenty hours a week, but she worked a forty-hour week. So we had her on the books as working a twenty-hour week and paid her double. She looked like she did four hours a day, but in fact she did a full shift. Anyway, we were visited by these blokes who said they were from the Home Office, and they came asking about her. Fortunately, she wasn't in that day, but they said they wanted a photocopy of everyone's passport faxed over, including hers, but they forgot to give us a fax number. We left it alone for a couple of days, did nothing and they never came back. Mind you, neither did the chambermaid.

The night cleaning staff are nearly as glamorous or exotic. We have Moroccans, Kenyans, and a few Iraqi Kurds, but they're mainly Bangladeshis. Forget what I said earlier about the chambermaids: the back-of-house guys have the worst job in the hotel. They do a 11:00 P.M.–7:00 A.M. shift, during which time they scrub the kitchens, clean all the silver, wipe down all the floors, clean the staff toilets, and do all the washing up. And they hate their job. In a business that thrives on tips to compensate for poor wages, there is no chance of a single spare pound coin coming their way. For, not only are they not allowed to interact with the guests, they're not allowed to be seen in any public area at all.

You can understand why morale is low, and they're always slacking off. They will disappear off to sleep anywhere. It is quite extraordinary. The other day I found a bloke squeezed into one of the lockers in the staff room having a nap practically standing up. When I worked at The Savoy, I used to have to do these great tours of all the subterranean passages under the Thames to make sure none of them were asleep on the job. Here it's a bit easier, as the hotel is smaller, but there are still loads of places for them to sleep—all sorts of nooks and crannies. It is difficult to keep track of everyone.

I bend forward and tug at my trouser leg, the congealed blood and material peel off my knees. The cleaner immediately understands what I am looking for. He takes me along another corridor and opens up a cupboard full of thin, badly made, black trousers. I smile and thank him before he disappears off into the dark. After about five minutes spent rifling through the shelves, I come up with a slightly shiny pair of trousers that look as though they might fit. Walking back along the maze of corridors, I find the kitchen, I poke my head around the door and find it almost empty except for a couple of cleaners slopping down the floor and another pair washing out the industrial mixers and large cooking pots.

Thankfully, the staff locker room is empty as I strip down to my underwear. The trousers are made of cheap material that starts to itch almost as soon as I get them on. I fold up my own suit trousers and put them in a Sainsbury's bag in my locker. I've still got a photo of my ex-girlfriend in there, I notice; I suppose I should really take it down. I have no idea how I'm going to clean those trousers. I'll take them to the dry cleaners, I should think, and charge it to the hotel.

On my way back upstairs I bump into the Rentokil man. This place is riddled with vermin and it's his job to hinder their spread, and make sure the guests never notice quite how many rats, mice, and roaches are a few yards from their feet.

"Evening," he says, as he approaches, a cage in each hand. He must be off to bait the traps just outside the kitchens.

It's normally the cleaners' job to keep an eye on the rattraps to see if we've managed to catch any of the little furry fuckers during the night. But the Rentokil bloke comes once a week, after service hours when the place is quiet, to check up on their positions, to rebait the traps and work out if we have any great infestations. I remember a terrible bedbug plague in a place where I used to work. They came in hidden in someone's suitcase, and they'd gone all the way through the hotel in a matter of days. You'd be amazed how few guests actually complained. A couple, covered in bites, did come to Reception and say something. But we were told to deny all knowledge of them. We just shook our heads, looked worried and rather confused. It seemed to do the trick until we got the problem under control.

But in the big hotels it is almost impossible not to have a vermin problem, mainly because they are so large and so old, with plenty of places for them to breed. Before their re-fits I have seen mice dancing along the baseboards of the dining areas in Claridge's while I was serving afternoon tea and the rats at The Savoy were a nightmare: situated right by the river, half of The Savoy is under ground and runs back underneath the Thames, so the place used to be crawling with them. It was a continual problem that they constantly fought to keep under control. There are cockroaches in pretty much every hotel that I have ever worked in. It's only good chambermaid work that keeps them out of the bedrooms.

"How are you this evening?" I ask, as he comes closer. I don't know the bloke's name but I know that he has been killing vermin here for over five years.

"Busy," he says, shaking both the cages. "Very busy. We've just caught a big brown rat in the wine cellar." He smiles. "So I'm off to reset the trap."

"Good." I smile right back. "That's excellent."

"Yeah," he sniffs. "Anyway, see you."

"See you," I reply, my toes curling slightly when I peer into the cages as he goes past.

"Oh," he says, stopping and turning around. "You'd better get back up there as soon as you can. I think the fire alarm has gone off."

"Fire alarm? But I can't hear anything down here."

"I know," he sniffs again. "That's no good in the event of a fire, now, is it?" he says, walking off in the opposite direction from the nearest exit.

I come rushing up the stairs, in my itchy, scratchy new trousers that are slightly too tight in the thigh, to find Dennis and André having a stand-up row in Reception. The fire alarm is blaring out at full volume, but no one seems to be paying any attention. Rather like a car alarm on a city street, it inspires curiosity but absolutely no sense of imminent danger and/or panic. I remember when The Savoy Theatre was actually on fire, it took us a while to persuade the guests to leave their rooms. This time, only a party of drinkers react. They walk out of the bar, their beverages still in hand, and they are standing around in the foyer with an expectant look on their faces. Not even Patrick, who I thought might be flustered and flapping like a neurotic, seems to be paying the loud siren noise any attention.

"We've asked you to do something about this before," I

can hear Dennis shouting at André. "It's your fault, your responsibility—you're duty manager tonight."

"Fuck you!" says André, unwisely giving Dennis a little shove with his white hand. "I can't keep my eye on everything and everyone all the time."

"It is your bloody job!" yells Dennis, shoving him rather forcefully right back.

"OK," I say, approaching at speed. "Where's the fire? What is going on?"

The screeching siren noise is enough to make anyone on edge.

"It's a false alarm," bellows Dennis above the noise. "And it is all because this little arse—"

The fire alarm suddenly turns itself off. Everything falls silent. Only the scream of "arse" reverberates around Reception. Everyone looks at Dennis. A couple of guests have open mouths.

"Hole," he finishes weakly. "This arsehole," he whispers, with a fat jab of his finger in the general direction of André. "This arse keeps insisting that is it all right to cook a fucking crêpe suzette underneath a fucking smoke alarm! How many more fucking times? You fucking cretin!"

"Cretin?" asks André. "What is this 'cretin'?"

"Arsehole! Idiot! You!" says Dennis, pulling moron faces as he does so. "Honestly," he says, turning towards me. "I fucking ask you—"

"Yes, well," I say, scratching the side of my neck. "Well, at least the alarm has stopped."

"Yeah," sighs Dennis. "Thank heaven for fucking small little mercies."

"We should brace ourselves for the arrival of the fire brigade," I say, looking anxiously out the front of the hotel.

"Shit, you're right," says Dennis, raising his voice again. "OK, everyone!" he says. "There is nothing to see here. Everyone back; back to the bar, and enjoy your drinks! Back to the bar, please, everyone, Gino is waiting for you!"

Too right he is, I think: Gino's bound to be pissed off. That's a good ten minutes of prime-time customers that André's cost him. It is almost worth coming in tomorrow just to hear the shouting in the morning meeting.

My heart sinks. Shit. I can hear the noise of the fire engines approaching; there are at least three engines on their way here. Obviously, no one from the hotel has telephoned them yet to tell them that is it a false alarm. Of course they haven't: it's my bloody job to do it!

The sirens are getting closer. Fuck. It sounds like there are four of them. That's another two thousand we'll be shelling out to the London Fire Brigade this month.

Every time a hotel has a false alarm they have to pay out, from £750 a time (for a small 100-room hotel), plus £250 for each fire engine. You can hardly blame them: every hotel call the fire brigade gets has to be treated as a potentially enormous disaster in the making. There are bedrooms of guests that have to be accounted for; there are dining rooms full of people who've had rather too much wine. You can imagine the hell if the fire were real, so the London Fire Brigade tends to take us seriously. They always send multiple engines and they usually arrive within fifteen minutes of the alarm going off.

They screech around the corner, and slam on the brakes. I contemplate running outside, waving my arms to tell them there's no fire and no need. But then I think I might well look like a traumatized fire victim escaping the inferno and it would only encourage them. So I stand still and wait for the scenario to unfold.

In a matter of minutes, they sprint through the front doors, helmets on, hoses at the ready, looking for the action. A man who looks like he is in charge heads up the first wave. His steps slow down as he takes in the image of Dennis, André, Patrick, and me, all staring at them.

"Oh, right," he says, grinding to a halt.

"It's a false alarm," I say, trying not to sound sheepish.

"Oh, OK," he says, raising his arm behind, halting the rest of his troops.

"Yes." I smile. "Sorry about that," I add, rather weakly. "It was a mistake."

"Right." The fireman nods. "We'll have to make an inspection of the building just to make sure."

"Yes, right, of course," I say. "It was a crêpe suzette in the dining room that started it all off."

"Right," he says, staring at me like I am speaking Greek. "The dining room?" he suggests.

"Yes," I nod. "André will take you."

André springs into action. The idea of escorting such a handsome man, in such a tight navy T-shirt, into the dining room, clearly gives him the biggest thrill he's had all evening, or even possibly all week. He sets off with a huge spring in his stride. The reaction to the fireman arriving in the bar is the same. The loud cheer that accompanies their entrance makes it all the way to Reception. Well, at least we've made their night. You never know, maybe we'll make up the £2,000 we have to give the fire brigade in the bar.

With all the distraction, I almost don't notice the Sheikh walking through Reception in his long white robes all on his own. I wonder where he's off to at this time of night.

"Good evening, sir," I say quickly, as he walks out into the street. He doesn't bother to react, just carries on walking, through the revolving doors and into his black, chauffer-driven Mercedes.

My telephone goes.

"Reception," I say.

"Hello," comes a slightly breathless voice.

"Yes."

"This is Room 233," he says.

"Right. How can I help you, sir?"

"Can someone go and get me some condoms?" he asks, in a voice that is devoid of embarrassment.

"Condoms?" I say. Dennis pricks up his ears.

"Yeah. A packet of three."

"Right. Any particular size or make?"

"No, um, yes, um, extralarge," he says. "Ribbed."

"Extralarge and ribbed," I repeat. Dennis rolls his eyes and opens the left-hand drawer of Tony's desk. It is packed with condoms of various sorts, but mainly extralarge and ribbed, which, for some reason, is one of the more popular ones on order. Dennis pulls out a packet and waves it at me. "Right, sir," I say. "We'll do our best. But you know . . ."

"Well, you know, if you have any problems," he adds suddenly, "any old condom will do."

"OK, sir," I say.

"You bastard!" says Dennis, after I hang up.

"I know." I smile. "It's just that, two minutes ago, the whole hotel was supposed to be burning down and all this guy can think of is sex. Anyway, I just hate the idea of people having lots of sex when I clearly am not."

"Oh, right," he says, clicking his fingers like he's just remembered something. "I'd forgotten you'd been dumped."

"Yeah," I say. "From a great height."

"Happens to the best of us," he says. "I hear Gavin is getting divorced."

"What, Deputy Manager Gavin?"

"The very same."

"Oh," I say, not knowing Gavin that well.

"The same reason as all of us," continues Dennis. "Long hours. Apparently he was never home."

"Tell me about it."

"Yeah, right." Dennis nods. "Do you want to go and get some coffee or something?"

"I might just go and check on how Gino is doing, if you know what I mean."

"Yeah, sure," he says. "Oi, Patrick," he yells across Reception. "Take these rubbers to Room 233. I hear the bloke's dying for them."

I walk into the bar, and it is heaving. Gino looks the picture of happiness, doing his cocktail thing; even grumpy old Gianfranco has a smile on his face. The fireman effect seems to have worked, and everyone's knocking back the booze. I spot Mr. Masterson sitting in the corner, with a hand on each of his prostitutes' knees. The girls have got a bottle of Dom Perignon Oenotheque Vintage 1988 (£270 a bottle) between them, but Mr. Masterson, to Gino's obvious delight, is on doubles of 1919 Dalwhinnie whiskey (at £150 a shot). I'm watching, leaning on the door, thinking about taking another Pro-Plus caffeine pill when Gino spots me, and beckons me over.

"Hello," he says, coming out to greet me. His lips are smiling, but his eyes are indicating a blonde on a stool. "I think we might have a problem here," he says, putting his arm around my shoulder, as he whispers in my ear. He directs me towards the blonde at the bar.

The blonde does indeed look a little the worse for wear. I saw her this morning when I checked her in with her husband, and I know they had dinner together in the hotel, but for some reason, she has been left to drink on her own.

"Good evening, madam," I say. I always start out politely.

"Oh hello," she replies. Her eyes are clouded with alcohol and her white silk shirt is undone a button too low.

"Are you having a good evening?"

"Apart from being left on my own by my shit of a husband,

who has gone to some shitty business meeting, I'm fine." She pauses and smiles. "In fact, since you've turned up, things are much improved."

"That's good, madam," I reply. It is always best to respond nicely to a flirter, especially a drunk one, as there is no telling what they might do. She drains her drink and stands up a little unsteadily. "Are you thinking of calling it a night, madam?" I ask.

"I'm thinking of ordering some coffee in my room," she says, with a relaxed smile. "Will you bring it up to me?"

This is, I have to say, not really my job, but Dennis is in Reception and there might possibly be twenty quid in it: there's no tipper like a pissed tipper. And if I'm here all night, I may as well make the most of it.

"Of course," I say, with a smile. "I'll be up right away."

I ring downstairs to the kitchen, wake up the lazy bloke in Room Service again, and order up a pot of coffee and some homemade shortbread to be delivered just outside the bar. Gino gives me a shot of vodka while I wait, and he doesn't ask me to pay. He mutters something about not having to go through another stock check for a while. The Room Service bloke brings up the tray and I take it up to her room myself. I knock on the door.

"Come in," she says.

I walk in, holding the tray and nearly drop the whole bloody thing. Jesus Christ! She is lying there, stark naked on the bed. Oh Lord! I don't know where to look, I don't know what to say, I can feel my whole fucking face going bright fucking pink. I've been propositioned by guests before, but nothing like this.

Sex between staff and guests is strictly forbidden, although it does certainly go on. I've never done it myself. It's far too risky, particularly if they're drunk. They might well regret it in the morning and if you're the guy who's taken advantage of a drunk guest, there's no knowing what might happen. It's not a good look; it is also a sackable offense. So, even though it is difficult to ignore a naked woman, flat on her back—laid out like a starfish—I do just that.

"Where would you like the coffee, madam?" I force myself to ask, just managing to get the words out.

"Over there." She points, propping herself up on her elbow.

"Right you are, then," I say, putting it down on the round table at the foot of the bed. "Um," I say, looking at the thickness of the shag pile on the floor and clearing my throat. "Will there be anything else?"

"Well," she says. I keep staring at the floor. "No."

"Good evening, then," I say, as I leave the room quickly, closing the door behind me.

Just as I walk a step away from the door, I hear her scream, "Fuck you!" And there is an almighty crash, as I presume she hurls the coffee and the tray against the door. I'm not quite sure what to do. Should I go back into the room and help clear up? Should I tell one of the night staff? I stand there for a second, and decide I'm probably the last person she wants to see right now, so I run back down to Reception to share what's just happened with Dennis. And while Dennis pisses himself with laughter, I ring up the Room Service night staff and tell one of them to go upstairs to clear up the mess.

The traffic through Reception is beginning to calm down, but I still have to keep an eye on who is going and who, more importantly, is coming into the hotel. Any passing tramp would give his eyeteeth for a nice cozy night in our establishment. They are always trying to slip past us, which is why, from now on, we keep watch on the door and take regular tours of the hotel, just to check to see if any of them have managed to find themselves a comfortable fire escape to bed down in. They also have rather a nasty habit of finding the Honor Bar and relieving it of all its alcohol. I think I might send Dennis on a quick tour of the place when he gets off his cell phone and finishes telling his long-winded joke at my expense. Dennis is better at dealing with tramps than I am: he's quite tough and unafraid, whereas I always end up feeling sorry for them. I always have half a mind to give them their fistful of wine miniatures, only I know it would come out of my wages.

I'm feeling exhausted. The shot of vodka has only gone halfway to reviving me. My legs are warmer and my cheeks feel like they have a bit more color, but the rest of me feels like it might spontaneously collapse at any minute. I can't believe that André set the fire alarm off with a crêpe suzette. He's been warned about using too much brandy in the past; Adrian is going to be so pissed off tomorrow morning.

I smile. Two fireman come back through the glass doors; their jackets are open and they have wide smiles on their faces.

"Bloody hell." One smiles at me. "Your bar's a laugh."

"Yeah." I smile back. "All done then?"

"Yup," says the other guy. "We're the last two out. It was definitely the pancake, mate, that set the whole thing off. The plastic cover's been singed on the smoke alarm and everyone in the dining room saw the blast from the brandy flames."

"Right." I nod.

"Everywhere else is fine," nods the first.

"OK then. Sorry to get you lot out here for no reason."

"Not to worry," says the second one. "We enjoyed seeing the fit birds in the bar."

"Good. So it was worth it."

"Definitely," says the first, tapping the side of his nose. "Quality."

"Good night."

"Night," they reply.

I'm about to get Dennis off his cell phone to go on tramp watch when my telephone goes.

"Hello," comes a distinctly drunken-sounding voice. "This is Room 412."

"Good evening."

"Now listen," he starts. "I have been calling Room Service for what seems like ages, and I've been transferred to you. I'd like a bottle of champagne."

"Right, sir," I say. "They're probably very busy down there." I'm going to kill that sleeping bastard.

"OK then," slurs the voice. "Right . . . what I would like is a bottle of your finest champagne!"

"Our finest?" I say. I can hear a girl giggling in the background. This man clearly wouldn't notice if I brought up a bottle of Asti in a bucket.

"Your finest!" he repeats.

"Well, we have bottles of very fine champagne that range from about £270 a bottle to a 1959 Dom Perginon Vintage for £1,450."

"Oh," he says, suddenly sounding less expansive. "A bottle of Veuve Clicquot would be nice."

"Vintage?"

"No," he says very quickly.

"That'll be £65."

"OK," he says. "That sounds fine."

"I'll get one sent up to your room immediately, sir."

I ponder for a second about doing it myself, but I think I've had enough drunk encounters at the moment so I dispatch Patrick, telling him that the punter is pissed and he might get a nice tip.

I've always found this time of night rather amusing when it comes to Room Service. Once people have a few drinks inside them, they start ordering the most extraordinary and expensive things. I have lost count of how many buckets of caviar have gone upstairs after midnight, only to be found by the chambermaids in the morning, barely touched.

Like the rather rich Arab guy at The Lanesborough one night, who ordered up a £5,000 magnum bottle of Chateau Petrus. It is an amazing wine that had been in the wine cellar for bloody ages, and it had become a standing joke that the sommelier had been itching to sell it. Anyway, he takes it up to the room; he opens it up with a flourish, and serves it as if it were liquid gold; he is careful not to waste a single little drop. He is thrilled, as he's finally managed to get rid of it, and the management will be delighted that they've got their money back. There are five people in the room, and he pours each of them a glass. Then he leaves, only to come back five minutes later, just to make sure that they are enjoying this fantastic and amazing wine. He knocks on the door, and expects to find them all in raptures, instead he walks in and finds this woman pouring cold Perrier water into his incredible 1947 Chateau Petrus, destroying the whole point of it all. The poor man walked straight out of the room and nearly burst into tears: it was priceless. He was in a bad mood for almost a week.

Dennis finally gets off his telephone.

"Oh, God," he says, whipping a tear away from his eye. "They loved your story at The Savoy." He starts to chuckle. "Honestly, I haven't had a laugh like that in a while."

"Well, I'm glad I can be of service," I say sarcastically.

"Keep your hair on," he says.

"Would you go and have a look around for tramps?" I ask. "What with the fire alarm going off and everything, you never know who might have managed to slip past us while we were otherwise occupied."

"Yeah," he agrees, getting up from behind his desk. "You're right. My mate at Charlotte Street has had a few problems already tonight."

That reminds me, there are some great stories about fights around Christmastime. People behave so badly in the run-up to Christmas, it is amazing. It is a time of total debauchery and madness. People throw up underneath tables and put a napkin on it, hoping that we won't notice. They pass out in the street, as soon as they leave the place. They piss in plant pots. It is extraordinary.

Anyway, some film director was in Charlotte Street having dinner, and there was someone sitting at another table who said something to the director and started a bit of an argument. The film director got up and threw the table in the air; he flew at this guy and head-butted him, and everyone else joined in.

One of the Spice Girls was there, sitting at a table, and she hit her panic button; all four of her security guards piled into the restaurant from their car outside. Everyone else left as quickly as they could; the chefs came out (as it has an open-plan kitchen) to try and break the fight up; the police were called. The diner who started the whole thing had his nose broken. There was blood all over the chefs' whites, smashed glasses everywhere. It was like being in a film; it was fantastic.

"So what's happened over there tonight?" I ask Dennis, as he walks towards the stairs.

"Oh, a couple of drunks in Reception," he says.

"Oh," I say, a little disappointed.

Dennis disappears off upstairs on tramp watch. I've asked him to have a look in on the Honor Bar on his rounds as well, just in case we have a sleeper in there. Sleepers are another one of those hotel nightmares that we have to deal with on the night shift.

They turn up everywhere. Slumped in the corridor, curled up on a sofa, leaning against the fire exit doors; guests too drunk to make it to their bedrooms pass out wherever they fancy, and lie there, dead to the world. You can't presume that they have keeled over anywhere near the room they are supposed to be staying in. They can be found on any floor, and in any area of the hotel: there is usually no rhyme or reason for them being where you find them. I've seen perfectly respectable businessmen lying flat on their backs covered in an explosion of dry roasted peanuts, passed out over the threshold of their own rooms, with their wallet and all their worldly belongings on display for any passing thief. And it's not just the guests; punters in the bar will take a wrong turning on the way back from the toilet, see a handy sofa and snuggle down for a snooze. Sometimes we don't discover them until the next morning, when they arrive in the dining room, complete with crumpled suit, and rather sheepishly ask for breakfast.

My telephone goes.

"Hello, Reception," I say, with as much zing and fizz as I can muster, which is very little.

"Hello," comes another drunken slur. "I can't get any porn," he moans.

"Porn, sir?" I say. "Oh dear. What sort of porn were you after?"

"Um, on the telly."

"Right," I say breezily. "You have to pay for that, sir."

"Yeah, I know that," he says, like I was some sort of moron.

"OK." I try to control my annoyance at being abused by a drunk porn-seeker at 1:15 A.M. "Do you have your remote control near you?"

"Yeah."

"Good. OK now, right, I'd like you to press the 'O' on the remote." I speak very slowly, like I'm talking to a child.

"Yeah," he says. Then there's a pause, and I can hear him looking for it. "Where is it?"

"At the bottom of the remote."

"Yeah." He starts to breath heavily, he is concentrating that much. "Got it."

"Good. Right, now press it."

"Yep."

"And there you will have a choice of things to watch that have come up on your screen; scroll down, make your choice, and press the red button," I say.

"Hang on, hang on," he says crossly. The message is clear.

Never stand between a drunk and his porn. I repeat my instructions. "Good, right," he says, as he hangs up.

"Thank you!" I say loudly down the phone. "Jerk."

A group of three girls, with not very many clothes on, walk through Reception.

"Excuse me," I say. "Can I help you?"

"Room 450," says one of them, as if it were absolutely none of my business.

"Fourth floor," I say.

"Yeah, thanks," says another, with heavy teenage sarcasm.

They stand around by the elevator, waiting for it to descend. It arrives, makes the sound of a microwave, the doors open, and out pops Dennis with the biggest grin on his face that I've seen in ages. He lets the ladies into the elevator and comes out, practically at a jog.

"Jesus Christ," he says, his face flushed with hilarity, his eyes watering with humor. "You won't fucking believe what I've just seen."

"What?" I say.

"Un-fucking-believable," says Dennis, rolling his eyes. "The cheek of the girl."

"What?"

"Honestly."

"Fucking what?"

"Well," he starts. "You know you told me to go and check out the Honor Bar? Right?"

"Yes."

"Well, I turn up there, and guess what I saw?"

"No idea. Absolutely no idea."

"Two people at it like bloody dogs," he declares.

"What?" I am admittedly a little shocked.

"Yeah. He's sitting on the green sofa, his trousers round his ankles while she's riding him like a rodeo rider, skirt around her armpits, underwear and tights in a pile on the floor. Her back-side's bouncing up and down ten to the fucking dozen."

"Shit," I say.

"No shit." He smiles. "Can you believe it?"

"What did you do?"

"Well, I coughed a couple of times, but they didn't seem to notice, then I said, 'I'm terribly sorry. I'll come back in a couple of minutes.' And then, get this, she turns around and says, 'Can you make it ten?'"

"No!"

"Too fucking right." He nods.

"What can you say to that?"

"Nothing," he shrugs. "So I came back in ten minutes and they're gone."

"Amazing." I start to laugh. "But it doesn't come close to that elevator woman."

"Shit, yeah," he says. "Who could forget her?"

Less than a month ago, Dennis and I had to deal with a woman who was extremely drunk and flirty in the bar. She was fine for a while, if a little leering, but Gino wasn't too pleased. So I escorted her out of the bar, and she then went to the toilet, and completely disappeared. About half an hour later, when Dennis was escorting someone else to their room, he discovered the woman having sex with another guest on the floor just outside the elevator. He tried tactfully to move them on, but they were having none of it. So we decided that, as it was late, we would leave them to get on with it, as they'd soon get bored and go back to their separate rooms. About ten minutes later, I spotted her husband coming back into the hotel. Dennis cleverly re-membered that his wife was still having sex outside the elevator on the third floor. I took it upon myself to delay the husband, while Dennis sprinted up three flights of stairs to decouple the wife. It was extraordinary. We probably saved their marriage, and she didn't even bother to thank either of us, or even tip us, when she checked out, looking pretty bloody hungover, the next day. Some people are so bloody rude.

Another group of young people come through Reception. They look half-drunk already.

"Excuse me," I say. "Can I help you?"

"No thanks," says one of the young men. "We're going to see a mate who is staying here."

"Really?"

"Yeah," he says back. "Room 450."

"Room 450," I repeat.

"Yes," giggles a girl. "It's his birthday."

"Fine." I really can't be bothered to argue.

Dennis is back on his cell, chatting away to some relative or other, telling them the Honor Bar shag story: the girl in the story is already asking for fifteen minutes more time. I guarantee by the end of the night she'll be having sex for a good half an hour. Honestly, I don't know how that bloke gets the energy to chat all the time. I wonder what he and his mates actually talk about whenever they do meet up, because Dennis has told them every story he's ever known before he sees them. Or perhaps they never meet up at all: they just have a relationship on the telephone and never actually see each other.

I envy his phone calls sometimes. Half the problem with this job is not the long hours, the rubbish pay, and the drunken abuse that you get, but the boredom of it all. Trying to keep awake while your body is craving sleep is a lot bloody harder if you are bored rigid. There really are only so many times I can watch Patrick rub down the brass door plates, or polish up the luggage trolley. I swear to God, every time he uses that bloody thing to take some sod's bags upstairs, he comes down and gives it a quick polish; I think he'd shag the thing if he could.

Jesus, I'm beginning to be a little irritable. Poor Patrick; if he wants to rub his trolley down all night, then it's up to him, and I should let him get on with it. I think I might go and check on Gino to see if he needs help getting rid of a few more vodka shots that might be cluttering up the bar.

The smell of cigar smoke is overpowering as I come into the bar, but it's a bit quieter now. Most of the hotel guests have gone to bed, leaving behind the hard core and the too drunk to move from their chairs and of course, Mr. Masterson and his two prostitutes. He seems to be having a whale of a time. Sucking on his Trinidad Diplomatic, feeling up his women, the beaming grin on his face is visible right the way across the room. One of the girls has certainly had a bit too much champagne. Her red silk chiffon top is slipping so far off her shoulder that it looks like her left breast is going to pop out at any moment. She doesn't seem to notice or care; either that, or it is part of her seduction technique.

Gianfranco, Alfredo, and Francesco are all starting to clear up, wiping down the tables, clearing up behind the bar, chucking away half lemons and limes. Gino is out from behind his bar, he is standing leaning forward, his hands clasped on the back of a chair, talking "Liquid History," or very expensive drinks, with a rather well-oiled-looking gentleman whose flushed cheeks match the color of his socks. Even from here, I can see that Gino is going in for the kill. It's the pseudorelaxed pose and the terrible jolly smile that give him away; it is only matter of time before I hear the suggestion that the customer try the £750-a-shot Napoleon cognac.

"Seven hundred and fifty pounds!" he splutters. There goes Gino: he can sniff out a sale from the other side of the bar. "It'd better be bloody great at that price."

"How about you, Mr. Masterson?" asks Gino, coming across the room and standing equidistant from the two of them. "Would you like to try a shot? It seems a shame to go down to the cellar and bring out this piece of history, if I have only one taker."

"What?" asks Mr. Masterson.

"Would you like to try some of my extra-special Napoleon cognac from 1796?"

"Oh right, too right I do," says Mr. Masterson, slapping someone else's thigh. "I remember that from last time. Isn't it about $1,000 a shot?"

"That's the one," says Gino.

"Fabulous," says Mr. Masterson. "Would my guests like to try some?" he asks the girls.

"Maybe just a bit," purrs one of the girls.

"Three glasses," says Mr. Masterson. "And make them doubles."

"Right away, Mr. Masterson," says Gino. He turns around and indicates that Gianfranco should get his arse down to the cellar as quickly as possible. He catches my eye and pretends to ignore me. I know there is no point in bothering Gino when he is in this mood; he is like some sort of tantric snake, luring them in with his hypnotic chatter about history, and luxury and the days of yore. I've seen him do this so many times before.

The bottle arrives, and he puts it in some special protective basket. He brings it to the table, where he will blow off the non-existent dust and gently caress the bottle with his hand. He then launches into a speech that starts with all the things that have been invented since this cognac was first made, and goes on to finish with the year of Catherine the Great's demise. The Americans love it; Gino's final thing is that he knows the population of America at the time it was made, which always sends them into the stratosphere.

I know for certain that I'm not going to get my shot of vodka at this precise moment, so I may as well go back to Reception and bide my time. I still have a long night ahead of me.

Dennis is back on his cell when I arrive. The Reception telephone is ringing.

"Hello, Reception," I say.

"Hello," comes this irritated and tired voice. "I can't sleep."

"I'm sorry to hear that, sir," I reply, thinking that makes two of us.

"There's a party going on in the next-door room," he continues. "Will you sort it out?"

"I'll send someone up right away, sir," I say.

This happens all the time. Guests book a suite, and before you know it, other guests start arriving, and you have a party on your hands. I'd thought there were a few too many people going up to 450, but I figured, if they don't make that much noise, it is not doing anyone any harm. Sadly, it seems I am wrong.

But, before I get Dennis off his cell phone, I make a quick call down to Room Service just to make sure that they're not ordering up a fortune's worth of stuff, because, believe you me, it makes a difference.

We had a just-married couple once at The Lanesborough, supposedly to start their honeymoon. They had a huge suite and, without telling the hotel, they actually had their wedding reception in the room. They had 60 people and ordered up room service. They ordered twenty-four bottles of Tattinger (at £49.50 a bottle) and some canapés. It was a full-blown party that went on till 5:00 A.M. There were complaints flying in from all over the hotel. But we chose to ignore them. Room Service said that, as they were ordering so much, we should let them carry on. In the end, we moved a couple of people to different rooms, and sent them up earplugs. But we were happy as pigs in the proverbial, as we were making a fortune. It is that age-old hotel motto, the more money you spend, the more you can get away with.

Celebrities do it all the time; I suppose, if you spend most of your life in hotels, then you do end up treating them as a sort of home away from home.

I remember one night at the Covent Garden Hotel, when

Johnny Depp and Kate Moss brought back a whole group of their friends. They'd booked the best suite in hotel. It is an amazing room: it's a massive loft suite, split over two levels. It is stunning, the bed is on the top level, and it overlooks a sitting room/ dining room area with fat sofas. It costs £1100 a night (including VAT). Anyway, they booked it for a Friday night, finally turning up after something else. They ordered thirty-six bottles of Krug, which, of course, the hotel didn't have enough of. We went crazy trying to get ahold of all this Krug, from any open bar, or club, or hotel all over the West End. They also ordered a whole load of stuff from the Room Service menu, and slowly but surely, all these people began to arrive, and they hosted this fuck-off party that went on all night. They spent a ridiculous amount, and, I think, they ended up with something like a £12,000 bill; it was crazy.

But I hear, in comparison to Miss Moss's recent thirtieth birthday party celebrations at Claridge's in the £4,000-a-night suite, it was a little tame. That bash seems to have set her back some £20,000, and she drank a loucher Louis Roederer, Cristal champagne (the 1994 version goes for £250 a bottle). Guests apparently partied till dawn, Sadie Frost showed her bosom to the press and there were rumors that it descended into some sort of wild party.

Unfortunately, tonight's lot in room 450 have only ordered up three bottles of Moët, which are hardly going to keep any of us in style. I finally manage to get Dennis off his bloody phone and tell him to get them to keep it down, otherwise, we'll throw all of the party-giver's guests out of the hotel. Dennis agrees, and doesn't seem to mind going upstairs again. I suspect he is hoping to find his dogging couple having sex somewhere indiscreet again. Instead, he is down and back in a jiffy.

"Piece of piss," he sniffs, as he walks across Reception. "As soon as I knocked on their door, they shut up. They're a bunch of kids out on Daddy's credit card," he surmises. "They won't cause us any trouble. In fact, after the drama of the first half of the night, I think we're going to be in for a quiet one," he says. "I can feel it in my bones."

Just as Dennis wanders back to his desk, a man in a Prince-of-Wales-checked suit with a briefcase, zigzags his way through the door towards the desk. "Looks like I spoke too soon," says Dennis, with a wink. "Incoming!" he adds, his hand cupped around his mouth.

"Good evening, can I help you, sir?" I say, as the man leans on Reception for support.

"The name's Jones, and I have forgotten my room number," he says, his breath toxic with alcohol.

"OK, sir." I smile. This is not a rare occurrence. "I'll check the computer."

Mr. Jones slumps over the desk. His eyes are red, his suit smells of cigars, his skin is sweating alcohol; he must have been out at some club. I run his name through the computer and come up with nothing. "You don't seem to be checked in sir," I say.

"What?" says Mr. Jones, jerking himself awake with his sudden head movement.

"You don't seem to be checked in," I repeat.

"Of course I'm check in," he slurs.

"Well, not according to the computer."

"Well, look again."

"I will, sir, but there really isn't any point."

"What do you mean, there isn't any point? Of course, there's a fucking point. I checked in here myself. Six hours ago. Look at the fucking computer again." Mr. Jones is starting to raise his voice and point his finger. The red veins on his nose engorge.

"I was on Reception six hours ago, sir," I continue. "And I'm afraid I do not remember checking you in."

"I don't care what you DO or, DO NOT fucking remember! My name is JONES! I am staying here! So give me my fucking ROOM KEY!" Mr. Jones is shouting so loud and so close to my face, that his acrid breath blowdries my hair.

"Well, I'm afraid we have no record of you being here," I say as calmly as I can.

"I don't care if you don't have a FUCKING record of me checking in. I checked in my FUCKING self, FUCKING six hours ago!"

"Are you sure, sir?"

"Are you calling me a FUCKING liar?" He slams his fist on the Reception desk. Dennis gets out of his chair and starts making his way to Reception. For a man who can't stand the sight of blood, he appears foolishly brave.

"Calm down, sir," he says.

"Calm down?" Mr. Jones spins round. "Who the FUCK are you?"

"I'm the doorman, sir," says Dennis.

"Well, you can FUCK OFF," shouts Mr. Jones, his hands on his hips. He turns back to face me. Slamming both hands down on Reception, he shouts again. "Give me my FUCKING room key."

"I'm sorry, sir, you don't have a room here," I explain again.

"I always have a FUCKING room at The FUCKING Dorchester!" he yells in my face. "Every FUCKING month. Almost every time I FUCKING come to London."

"Well, you may well still have one," I say. "Perhaps you should go to The Dorchester and find out."

"Oh?" says Mr. Jones, his body is rendered floppy with confusion. "I'm not at The Dorchester?"

"No, sir," I say.

"The Dorchester is up the road," nods Dennis, turning Mr. Jones gently in the direction of the revolving doors.

"Good," announces Mr. Jones defiantly, on his way out. "I'm glad, because I'd never stay in this place. It's a fucking SHIT HOLE!"

"Right you are, Mr. Jones," says Dennis, helping the door revolve. "Fuck off," he mutters at the glass, with a little polite wave.

Dennis is still doing his little polite wave when the Sheikh comes back into the hotel with a group of about six Gulf guys. They all look somewhat confused by Dennis's greeting, but they soon all walk off in the direction of the bar, their white robes and headdresses flowing after them.

I smile, wondering how Gino will cope with this. It is quite late for him, he usually likes to be off home at around this time. But the arrival of seven blokes from the oil-rich Gulf states is surely enough to make him put his coat back on the hook and line up his most expensive spirits. Having said that, I think he may well still be busy, as I'm sure I haven't seen Mr. Masterson leave the bar with his two prostitutes yet.

"Who are all those guys?" asks Dennis, as he sits back down at Tony's desk and starts playing with the drawers.

"No idea," I say.

"D'you think they're his mates?"

"No. They didn't look very matey."

"Businessmen?"

"Possibly."

"They're always doing business at odd hours, those guys. Their body clocks are wrong," says Dennis, picking fluff off his suit. "They get up at teatime, they eat cream teas for breakfast, they order dinner at 3:00 A.M.—they're mad."

He's right. Come August, all the luxury hotels in London are full to the brim with guys from the Gulf states. It is too hot in the Middle East in the summer, so the superaffluent move into The Lanesborough, The Dorchester, or The Savoy for the month, taking over suites and sometimes even whole floors. In fact, some places are so keen to keep their Arab clientele happy that they provide indoor barbecue kits for the rooms, as well as Arabic Room Service, where you can order up a whole baby lamb. Because the Arabs do like their midnight feasts.

It can be quite shocking. Once, one of the £2,500-suites rang up for water or something like that. I went up with my tray, knocked on the door and walked into the suite to find a dead sheep lying in the middle of the room. It had just been butchered, and there was blood all over the floor and all over the bathroom walls. The bath was full of blood where they had slit its throat. It was such a horrible and confusing sight that for a second I didn't know if they were going to fuck it, or eat it. It still had all its fur. But I presumed they were going to skin it and eat it. It was all very disturbing. Either way I didn't hang around to find out.

And it wasn't a one-time thing. Talking to mates in the industry, I heard of plenty more dead sheep in plenty more hotel suites, including the Four Seasons. But one thing I have always wondered about is how they ever get the sheep in the room in the first place? You would have thought that you'd notice a sheep trotting through reception on its way towards the elevator? But apparently not: of all the dead-sheep stories I have heard about, never once were they spotted coming into the hotel in the first place. It is surely one of life's great mysteries.

"What are you doing?" asks Dennis.

"Nothing," I say, putting three mints into my mouth at once. And I don't even like mints.

That's another thing, apart from the boredom of the job—the loneliness of it all. If only my girlfriend hadn't dumped me because I was doing too many night shifts, I might give her call around now. I used to enjoy doing that when we were going out. She'd talk to me in her sleep and forget that we'd ever had a conversation at all the next day. I used to find it amusing; I could tell her things that I knew she would never remember. But she got pissed off about being stood up at the last minute all the time. I don't blame her really: I wouldn't put up with it, if it weren't my job. So instead, I'm sitting here, with no one to call, wondering if I should take another pill. Will it keep me awake, or will it just make my heart race? My eyelids already feel like they've been stapled to the back of my head; I'm a lab-rat for a sleep-deprivation experiment. These are the hazards of doing nights; caffeine addiction and lack of sunlight; it's no wonder that we all look so goddamn pale.

Dennis is back on his phone again. He's rambling on to another one of his cousins, one who runs the door at another luxury hotel in town. From the few tidbits that I can pick up from over here, while obviously pretending not to listen, I gather that they've got some showbiz bash on in their ballroom; soap stars and some singers from one of those fake, reality TV bands are apparently wandering around like they own the place. Dennis's cousin has just had to stop some bloke from pissing into a plant pot. Dennis is laughing like he's never had to stop anyone relieving themselves in foliage before in his life.

It always amazes me how often guests seem to forget they are staying in a hotel and start treating the place like their own. Not that people piss in plant pots at home, but it is odd how some guests have no respect for the hotel's property. It is almost as if, since they've paid the money, they can do what they want, like break into the swimming pool for late-night swims. Guests always think that they are being so incredibly original: they start up the Jacuzzis, take all their clothes off, and have their own private pool parties. They have orgies, and group sex parties in the hot tubs, and all along, they think they are wild and wacky and fabulous—like no one's ever been there and done that before.

But actually, there are a few people who are a little different. Take Pamela Anderson and Tommy Lee, for example. They broke into the gym at The Lanesborough and had sex on the exercise bike, and then went on to use all other pieces of gym equipment in manners they were not really designed for. Unfortunately for them, they were filmed by the security cameras through the two-way mirror. They were there to protect the expensive gym equipment from theft, but they also recorded every single athletic move for the delight and delectation of the staff the next day.

"I think I might go and check on Gino," I say, finally swallowing my mints.

"What?" says Dennis, putting his hand over the telephone.

"I think I might go and check on Gino."

"Fair enough. I'm going to send Patrick off on tramp watch."

"Oh, good idea," I say, leaning around the corner, to see Patrick looking rather sleepy on his shiny brass trolley. "He looks like he is about to nod off."

"Oi, Patrick!" barks Dennis. The boy flinches. "Get your arse up, and check the hotel for tramps, drunks, or both." Patrick is up and off before anyone can say "You're fired," and he jogs up the first flight of stairs like his balls were on fire. "Keep an eye out for shaggers in the Honor Bar!" Dennis yells after him, before returning to his telephone call. "Sorry about that, mate," he says. "What? Didn't I tell you? Going at it like hammer and tongs, they were. I saw her arse and everything . . ."

Back in the bar, and the place is even thicker with cigar smoke. It seems that everyone left in the place is sucking on a Monte Cristo of varying length and thickness. Gianfranco, Alfredo, and Francesco all look exhausted. Their faces are white, their eyes red-rimmed and their skin looks tacky with old beads of sweat. They are leaning on the bar, their coats tucked under the shelf waiting for the signal to go home. Around them, the bar is immaculate, every glass shines in its place, every silver cocktail shaker is washed, dismembered, and laid out to dry on a tea towel. Only Gino is still working the bar for all he is worth. He hands out smiles and bonhomie to anyone who still wants to spend a lot of money on alcohol.

Mr. Masterson finally decides to call it a night. He gets unsteadily to his feet, using both his prostitutes for support.

"Gino!" he says, throwing a large hand in the air. "Come over here, my good man."

"Yes, Mr. Masterson," says Gino. "Would you like anything else?"

"I think I've had quite a lot already, Gino, don't you?" He chuckles and Gino joins in. "Here," he says, handing over £100. "Get something nice for your wife."

"Thank you, Mr. Masterson, very kind of you."

The bar boys snigger. Gino is no closer to having a wife than Victoria Beckham is to having a square meal. Only Mr. Masterson doesn't seem to have noticed.

"Excellent," he says, as he weaves his way towards the exit. "Good night, guys," he says to the Sheikh and his white-robed entourage. They mumble something incomprehensible in return. As he stumbles on towards the bar, he scrabbles about in his pockets some more and, pulling out a wad of cash, he proceeds to slip fifty-pound notes into the top pockets of Francesco,

Alfredo, and Gianfranco's jackets. That brings a bit of color back to their cheeks. He does the same to me, just because I am standing by the door. I think about saying something, but my earlier smug attitude towards his money is well and truly faded, along with the daylight and, if the man is drunk and wants to hand out his cash, who am I to argue? So I smile and say "Thank you" along with the rest of them.

The prostitutes, however, looked less than thrilled. The man is clearly too drunk to do it, so it doesn't look like either of them are going to make their full whack tonight. Their date's ability to throw his money about in every direction other than theirs, is also clearly beginning to annoy them.

"Come along now, Mr. Masterson," says one of them. "One step in front of the other."

"I am quite capable of walking, Woman," he snaps. "There is plenty of lead in my pencil yet," he announces, knowledgeably tapping the side of his nose. "Thanks to the joys of Viagra." He laughs and slaps the other prostitute on the arse and she hoots with delight. "Now," he says, grinding to a halt in the corridor. "Eenie, meanie, minie, mo," he says, his rather red finger going back and forth. "You!" he declares, falling forward a step. "You're the lucky one," he says, handing over a fistful of money to other girl, without even looking her in the eye. "Good night," he adds, bowing slightly. The rejected, dark-haired prostitute stomps off along the corridor, her high-heeled shoes slapping the marble as she goes. The other girl giggles conspiratorially and taking hold of the drunk's red hand, takes him off in the direction of the elevator.

I sigh: the scene depresses me. It's not as if I haven't seen it before, or that I won't ever see it again; but somehow, tonight it makes me feel down. Maybe it reminds me that we are all prostitutes in the luxury hotel business. We spend our whole life fawning around, being nice to arseholes, and more especially, rich arseholes, in the hope that they'll give us a tip. But then again, I think, as I feel my top pocket, fifty pounds is fifty pounds, and it's a hell of a lot more than those guys make downstairs.

Gino gives the bar boys the signal that they can go home. He only has the Sheikh's table to deal with, and it doesn't seem fair to keep them all on. The Sheikh is not being particularly demanding: he is playing cards and slowly working his way through a bottle of 1919 Dalwhinnie whiskey with his pals, smoking £175 Davidoff Number One Cuban cigars. Gino seems happy, it's all so reassuringly expensive.

Gianfranco, Francesco and Alfredo file out of the bar, beckoning me with them.

"Jesus fuck," says Gianfranco, stretching his arms in the air as he walks out of earshot. "That was a bloody shit of a day. I mean *figlio di puta*," he says shaking his head. "That stocktaking man."

"I know." Alfredo nods. "Bastard."

"Who wants a drink?" asks Francesco.

"God, I'd love one," I say. "But I'm afraid I'm on till 7:00 A.M."

"You poor bastard," says Alfredo, putting his arm around my shoulder, as we all walk through the glass doors into Reception. "Well," he smiles, pulling something out from underneath his jacket. "Your need is greater than ours," he says, handing me a half full bottle of tonic water.

"What's that?" I ask.

"Vodka." He smiles. "It's a little something I managed to get earlier."

"Thank you," I say, trying to hand it back. "But it's yours."

"No, man, don't worry." He pushes the bottle back towards me. "Thanks to Mr. American man, we can all drink well tonight."

"Who wants to go to Hombres?" asks Francesco, clearly desperate to let off steam.

"I'm knackered." Gianfranco shrugs.

"We're all knackered," says Francesco. "Come on!! It's only Oxford Street."

"OK," says Gianfranco. "One drink."

"One drink?" says Alfredo. "What the fuck is the point of one drink? You may as well have two."

"OK, two drinks, then," says Gianfranco.

"Two drinks?" laughs Alfredo. "What's the point of two . . ."

And the three of them disappear into the night, leaving me standing in Reception with a half a bottle of vodka and Dennis still talking on his cell phone.

I take the bottle of vodka into the back office and find a couple of old coffee mugs. Neither of them appears to be too dirty, so I pour the warm spirit into each of the mugs. I know I don't have to give Dennis any, but I also know that, if he had any alcohol on him, he'd do the same for me. I take over his mug of vodka to Dennis and he hangs up.

"What's this?" he asks, giving the mug a sniff.

"Vodka," I say.

"Doesn't smell like it," he says.

"That's because it's in a coffee mug," I explain.

"Oh, right," he says. "Cheers!" he adds, downing the whole thing in one. "Oh!" he sniffs. "That's much better." He smiles. "Thanks, mate."

"Don't thank me," I say. "It was Alfredo."

"I've always liked those Wops behind the bar. Good blokes, all of them."

"Yeah," I say, giving my mug a sniff.

"It's better down-in-one," he says. "There's a bit of a coffee aftertaste."

"Right," I say, knocking it back. "You're right. Tastes of Mellow Birds."

"I hate that coffee."

"So do I." I cough; my eyes are watering, but my throat feels warm and so does my stomach. "I think I'd better have look around downstairs, don't you?" I say, feeling suitably fortified.

"Yeah," agrees Dennis. "Where's that little shit, Patrick? He better not have found somewhere to doss down, the little bastard, otherwise he'll be out on his ear in the morning."

"I'll keep an eye out."

"See you in a bit. And thanks for the vodka."

"Pleasure," I say.

As I walk back down the stairs and into the depths of kitchen, I have to admit to being a little scared. I open each fire door with slightly more trepidation than the last.

I open the kitchen door; the place is so quiet. I say hello to the one guy who is still bleaching the kitchen floor, but he doesn't reply. I think him a little rude, but it is not until he turns his back entirely to me that I see he is wearing a Walkman.

I walk further on. The staff toilets are already clean; the grim rust-stained bowls are dripping with bright-blue liquid, and the bins have been emptied. There are a couple of men sitting and smoking in the staff room, but they stand up and stub out their cigarettes as soon as I walk in. I smile and say, "Good evening," but no one bothers to respond. They file past and get back to work. After they've gone, I check the lockers to see if anyone is asleep there: nothing. I go back and check the storerooms at the back of the kitchen, another favorite haunt for slackers. But I suppose word has got out that I'm about, and anyone who might have been sleeping is long gone. I'm too tired to bother checking out any of the more out-of-the-way places. The idea of wandering about in the dark trying to catch people out really does not appeal, particularly at this hour of the morning. So I go back upstairs to Reception.

"Nothing to report," I say to Dennis, who is reading one of Tony's pamphlets like he's never seen the thing before.

"Mmm," he says. "All quiet here, too."

Patrick finally wanders back down the main stairs. His steps are heavy, and he is looking a little drained.

"I have been along every corridor and looked in every doorway and I haven't seen anyone," he says, sounding exhausted.

"Oh, right," says Dennis, whose own tramp tour of the hotel takes about ten minutes and that's including a toilet break near the Honor Bar. "Very good. Do you want to go and get yourself some coffee from downstairs?" he suggests. "Sounds like you need it."

"Thank you very much," says Patrick, and shuffles off downstairs.

Dennis and I are left in silence; the hotel is quiet. Occasionally we hear a short volley of male laughter coming from the bar; it's hard to believe that Gino is still in there, serving away, smiling like a maniac with his knife caught in the toaster. Dennis starts to chuckle.

"What?" I say.

"What?" he says, right back.

"You started to laugh."

"I did?"

"Yeah. What were you thinking about?"

"Oh, God." He smiles. "That bloke from last week. Do you remember the guy who was so drunk that I had to help him up the stairs."

Poor Dennis almost had to carry the bloke upstairs, he was so drunk. Once up in his room, it was apparently chaos. The drunken bloke bent down to take his shoes off, lost his balance, and tried to grab hold of the curtain as he fell straight though the French windows and out onto the balcony. The doors shattered, and the curtain rail came down on top of him.

"It was a nightmare." Dennis chuckles. "The hotel was full and there was nowhere else to put him. D'you remember?" I nod and laugh at the same time. "The guest was fine, lying on the balcony, crying with laughter. He thought it was the funniest thing that had ever happened. The room was fucked, but the guest didn't care; in fact, he couldn't even speak, he just wanted to go to bed. So, in the end, we put the curtain rail back up and closed the curtains, and then dealt with it the next morning."

I smile. "Tony was bloody furious."

"Yeah." Dennis smiles. "I bet he ordered a new set of curtains as well as some new French windows on the bloke's bill."

"You can be sure of that."

"Yeah."

"Are you all right there on your own for a moment, Dennis?" I ask, standing up.

"Yeah." He looks at his watch. "The worst of it should be over by now. It's Nutter Hour next." He smiles. "All we need is Dressing Gown Bloke to come down the stairs."

"Yeah." I laugh and turn to go to the downstairs toilet. I look up: my heart sinks; I can see a man in a dressing gown slowly padding down the stairs.

"Oh, hello there," he says. "I'm afraid I couldn't sleep. I thought I might come downstairs and join you . . . for a bit of a chat."

There's nothing that ruins a night shift more than the arrival of the Dressing Gown Man: they are the bane of any sane receptionist's life. They plod down the stairs when you are at your most tired and often when you least expect it. They sit there, in their bloody slippers and talk you through their turgid lives. I've heard more life stories at three in the morning than any bloody shrink; at least they get paid to listen to people prattle on about their boring problems, their terrible childhoods, their sticky divorces, and their difficult teenage children. I've done it so many times now that I should really consider starting a counseling service.

"Good evening, sir," I say, my teeth gritting. "Can I get you anything? Like a drink from the bar? The cocktail bar is probably about to close but the Honor Bar is open."

"Oh no," says the Dressing Gown Man, all pious and abstemious. "I just thought I might sit here for a while, you know, seeing as I can't sleep."

"Right." I smile, jaw clamped tight. "Well, I'm just off to the toilet. But I'm sure Dennis will entertain you."

"Dennis?" says the man, turning towards Dennis.

"Yes, that's right," says Dennis, standing up and giving me a discreet finger with his left hand under the desk.

"Good," says the Dressing Gown Man, sitting down on the yellow chintz sofa next to Dennis's desk. He sits back and crosses his legs, giving me a quick flash of his bollocks as he does so. I do wish people would put underpants on when they come down to bore us with their insomnia. "Well, I'm Terrance, but my good friends call me Terry."

"Right, Terrance," says Dennis. "How long are you staying with us, then?"

"I've been here a couple of nights already," shares Terrance.

"Oh." Dennis nods. "Did you manage to sleep all right the other nights?" He asks in such a way that, if you didn't know him any better, you'd think that Dennis actually cared.

"Last night was alright," declares Terrance. "But I have to admit that Wednesday night, I was tossing and turning a bit."

"Oh, dreadful," says Dennis. "There is nothing worse, is there, than tossing all night, in bed, on yer own?"

I snort. I bite the skin between my thumb and forefinger to stop myself from laughing, and I decide it is better to leave the lobby quick sharp, before I collapse into a fit of laughter and take Dennis down with me. As soon as I am through the glass doors, I let out a howl, and walk off giggling to myself.

Downstairs, and the staff urinals, despite being recently cleaned, are as unsavory as usual. There's a constant dripping of some tap, or cistern, that no one ever remembers to repair. There's a cloying smell of urine, damp, and old cigarettes. There's water and possibly piss all over the floor, as well as the graffiti in about seven different languages, which I presume all say something like "Hell," or "Get me the hell out of here." It is not the sort of place that you want to dawdle in, or certainly take a nap. I can't face using one of urinals, so I open one of the cubicle doors; the locks have never worked as long as I have been here. I find one of the cleaners sitting down, his head leaning against the wall, fast asleep. He is wearing a pair of bright-yellow rubber gloves and he is holding a J-cloth, both of which are sitting neatly on his lap. He is dark-skinned, but perhaps a little pale to be a Bangladeshi. If I lean in and listen above the dripping water, I can hear him snoring. He looks relaxed, his mouth curls upwards underneath his mustache. I cough. He wakes with such a start that he leaps off the toilet seat, dropping his J-cloth to the floor.

"Oh my God, oh my God, oh my God," he repeats, panic-stricken, like I am about to hit him, or fire him, I can't work out which. "Please sir, please sir," he begs, his yellow hands flapping.

"Calm down," I say, stepping back out of the cubicle. "Calm down, mate, I only wanted a pee."

"Sorry, sorry," he says, looking and sounding confused. I'm not sure if he can understand English.

"I only wanted to use the toilet." I speak very slowly.

"I understand you," he says, equally slowly back.

"You do?"

"Yes, sir."

"There really is no need to call me 'sir,'" I say.

"OK, sir," he says.

"Where are you from?"

"Iraq."

"Oh."

"I'm from the North."

"Oh," I reply, as I look him up and down. "How long have you been here?"

"In the hotel?"

"Yes."

"Three months," he says. "But I work days in another hotel in Bayswater."

"Oh, right," I say.

"It is a three-star."

"Right." I nod. "How long have you been in the UK?"

"Eighteen months. I was a doctor before."

"A doctor," I say, sounding surprised.

"Yes." He nods. "But now I clean and change beds. I'm not complaining," he says, quickly.

"Yes, well. I'm sure not."

"No."

"Good." I smile. "Not long to go now till the end of your shift."

"No," he says.

"Then back home to your wife."

"She's still in Iraq."

"Oh."

"Good night," he says, as he walks past me and out the door.

"Good evening. Um . . ." And then I stop as I realize I didn't catch his name.

Halfway back upstairs, I can sense that Dennis is about to keel over with boredom. I can hear the monotone of Terrance's voice, punctuated by Dennis's curt responses.

"Really? . . . Really? . . . Is that right? Really?" he says. I can't believe that Terrance actually thinks he's listening. "Ah ha," he says, as I come through the doors. "There you are!" he says getting out of his chair, relief writ large all over his face. "I think I'd better pop off to the toilet myself."

"Oh, oh, right." Terrance nods. "Take as long as you want,

Dennis," he says, patting the yellow chintz sofa. "I'm not going anywhere."

"Oh, right," says Dennis as he walks towards me. "You shit," he whispers quietly in my ear as he goes.

"Alright there, Terrance," I say, as I stand back behind the desk.

"Oh fine," he says, mincing his buttocks into the sofa cushions. "He's very nice, your doorman."

"Yeah. He's been with us for years."

"So he said," says Terrance.

"Good," I say, looking down at the desk like I'm very busy indeed.

Just as Terrance inhales, ready to strike up another conversation, the Sheikh comes into Reception, accompanied by his card-playing entourage. Their arrival through the glass doors finally makes Terrance put a sock in it, as he sits and stares. The Sheikh kisses each and every one of his friends/colleagues/employees on both cheeks and escorts them to the front of the hotel. Patrick rushes forward and opens the door. The Sheikh waves them goodbye, hands Patrick a ten-pound note before turning to walk back towards the elevator.

"Good night, sir," I say, as he walks past.

"Good night," he replies.

"I hope you had a good evening."

"Very pleasant," he says, getting into the elevator. "A nice early night." He smiles, looking at his gold watch.

"Sleep well," I say, as the doors close.

Before Terrance can pick up his conversational baton once more and launch into 101 questions about who the Sheikh is, and where he comes from and how long he will be here (which I can see he is itching to do, and I mean that quite literally), my telephone goes.

"Hello," I say.

"Oh hello," comes this very chirpy, chatting voice. "I'm terribly sorry to have bothered you," he starts.

"Yes."

"But I have stayed in your hotel before . . ."

"Yes."

"And I was wondering if you could help me." He pauses.

"Um, if I can, I will," I say, wondering where this conversation is going.

"Good," he says. "Right. I've got this corn on the cob and I was wondering how I should cook it?"

"I'm sorry?"

"Well, I've got this corn on the cob, and I was wondering how I should cook it?" he repeats.

"Corn on the cob?"

"Yeah, that's right, corn on the cob. I mean should I panfry it?" he asks. "People are doing a lot of that these days. Aren't they?"

"Sorry," I say. "When did you say that you stayed here?'

"Oh, right," says the man. "God," he inhales. "That would be a couple of years ago now; I took my wife there for the weekend. We're divorced now. Hence the call, I suppose."

"Oh, right," I say. "Well, I wouldn't panfry it."

"You wouldn't?"

"No. I'm afraid I'm a bit traditional when it comes to corn on the cob. I'd boil it and then cover it in butter and pepper and eat it with my fingers." Terrance is looking at me like I have gone mad. Even Patrick is managing to look quizzical through his fatigue.

"Interesting," says the man, sounding impressed. "That sounds like a very good idea."

"Thank you," I say.

"No, thank you," he says. "You've helped me no end."

"Good." I smile. "Just as a matter of interest, I ask. You sound a bit far away, where are you calling from?"

"New York," he says. "Good evening, and thanks."

"Good evening." I hang up.

"That sounds like a weird phone call," says Terrance.

"Not really," I say, looking down at my desk again.

I'm not lying. We get odd culinary telephone calls all the time from guests past. They are usually ringing up to ask about some dish that is made in the kitchen here, that they are trying to re-create over there. Gino also does get an awful lot of cocktail calls: people, drunk or sober, asking him how to make a chocolate or raspberry martini. We've even had other restaurants call up and say they have a table of six demanding White Russians, or some-thing, just like we make here, and could we give them the recipe. More often than not we tell those sorts of people where to get off. If they want one of our White Russians, they should come here. But everyone else we try to help. Even the mad hostesses who ring up from their own dinner parties and ask for the recipe for a béchamel sauce or a champagne sabayon. I have talked so many not-so-domestic goddesses through making hollandaise sauce, I could make it in my sleep. But making people feel part of the hotel family is all part of the service.

Gino comes through the glass doors, navy coat on, with his cashmere scarf wrapped around his neck. He does his fake-stagger exhausted walk towards the front desk and flops his head for-ward.

"Good night?" I ask.

"Exhausting," he says.

"Oh, well."

"But . . ." He lifts his face, a triumphant smile beams up. "But," he says, "I made over eight hundred pounds in tips and managed to shift one bottle of that 1919 Dalwhinnie and half a bottle of the 1796 Napoleon cognac."

"Jesus."

"No," he replies. "Mr. Masterson, the Sheikh, and his friends from the Gulf."

"Well, you'll sleep well tonight."

"Well, I was going to have a couple of drinks to celebrate," he says. "Do you know where the others have gone?"

"Oh, shit," I say. "I'm sorry, I wasn't listening: Hombres or Samantha's."

"At least I shall enjoy looking." He grins. "Good night." He pulls his collar up. "See you tomorrow."

"I hope not," I say.

"See you anyway," he says, heading for the door.

Dennis comes in through the glass doors and Terrance shifts expectantly in his seat.

"Back so soon," I say.

"Yeah, well," sniffs Dennis, "I thought I'd check the kitchen for sleepers while I was down there and I found three of them asleep in the supply cupboards at the back. Scared the life out of them, I did. I told them to get some coffee and get back to work." He walks back towards his desk. "You still here, Terrance?"

"Oh yes," says Terrance. "Don't think I'll sleep for a little while yet."

Dennis sits back down at his desk and takes out some folder that has Tony's theater tickets in it. He picks up a pen, and makes as if he is very busy. Terrance's gaze wanders around the lobby, looking up at the enormous chandelier and over at the various potted plants that we have dotted around the place. He looks over at my desk, checking out the tropical flower arrangement.

"Those are fairly amazing," he says. "I wonder where—"

Thankfully, my telephone rings. I put my hand in the air. "I'm sorry," I mouth. "I have to take this. Reception?" I say.

"Oh hello," comes this very quiet, female voice. "You've got to help me."

"Of course, madam," I whisper back. "What can I do?"

"There's a man outside my room," she says. "He's knocking on my door. I think he wants to break in."

"Don't answer the door," I say.

"I have no intention of doing that," she hisses. "But will you send someone up, get the police, anyone, and make him go away."

"Right, madam, absolutely. I'm on my way."

"Hurry up. Please. Room 306."

"I'm on my way." I put down the phone. "I'm sorry," I tell Terrance. "There's a bit of an emergency on the third floor. Dennis," I say, as I leap out from behind the desk. "Some woman is saying there is a pervert outside her bedroom door, so I'm going up."

"OK," he says. "Do you want me to come, as well?"

"I'll call you if I need you."

"OK," he says, as I rush through the glass doors. I sprint up the front stairs, as it is so much quicker than waiting for the elevator.

Six flights of stairs later, I arrive on the third floor, completely out of breath. I must stop smoking, I think, as I walk along the corridor towards Room 306. You can't fight perverts if you're knackered when you get there. It's quite dark, walking along these corridors late at night. All the hall lights have been turned down to prevent the bright lights from going under guests' doors. My imagination is working overtime. I have an image of this huge hairy bloke, dressed in black, wearing leather driving gloves, waiting for me. Instead, as I turn the corner, I'm greeted by a sight that could only be described as a slightly larger version of Gollum from *The Lord of the Rings*.

"Jesus," I say, as I see him.

"Oh, thank God," says the small naked man, frantically trying to cover his genitals with his hands. "Thank God, you are here," he says, his large eyes imploring. "I've locked myself out of my room and I can't get back in."

"Sorry?" I say. I have to admit that I am a little stunned. This small naked man is not what I was expecting.

"I got up in the middle of the night for a pee," he says. "And I walked out the wrong door, and before I realized my mistake, the door closed behind me. And now no matter how hard I knock, my wife won't wake up."

"Oh right," I say, the whole situation making itself clear. "What's your room number?"

"308," he says.

"I'm afraid, sir, you have been knocking on the wrong door, which might explain why your wife would not wake up. You see, you have been frightening the lady who is sleeping next door to you."

"Oh Lord," he says, one of his hands reaching for his mouth. He immediately regrets it. "Oh Lord, what a business."

"Don't worry, sir," I say, reaching for my pass-card. "You get to bed, sir, and I'll explain the situation to the lady next door."

I let him into his bedroom, and try to talk to the woman next door. It takes me a good three minutes before she will open the door for me. And when I do, the poor thing is so distressed that she bursts into tears, and puts her arms around me. It transpires that the naked man has been knocking on her door for the last half hour, and she has been getting progressively more frightened and increasingly desperate. I tell her if she is worried another time, she should call immediately. I then suggest she get herself a brandy from the minibar to help her unwind a little more, and she smiles. I think, she thinks she now looks a little foolish, but you could hardly blame her for panicking.

Back downstairs again, and Dennis is still talking to Terrance. No amount of pretending to look busy is going to put the man off his chatting.

"Alright, then?" asks Dennis, as I come out of the elevator.

"Fine. The pervert turned out to be a naked man locked out of his room."

"Oh right," says Dennis. "One of those."

"Except," I add. "He was also knocking on the wrong door, trying to get in."

"Shit," says Dennis. "I bet that scared the living daylights out of the person next door."

"Yeah," I say. "She was a little shaken up."

"I bet that sort of thing happens all the time?" Terrance laughs.

"No, not really," says Dennis. "That sort of thing is actually quite rare."

"Oh," says Terrance. "How very interesting."

"Mmm," says Dennis, picking up a booklet on walking in the Peak District.

Terrance gets up out of his seat and smooths down his dressing gown. Dennis is looking at him out of the corner of his eye; his body is tensing with expectation, as Terrance moves in the direction of the stairs. I'm watching him as well. I can sense that we are both willing him to go upstairs, desperate for him to fuck off and leave us in peace. Terrance has his hands in his pockets, as he looks one of the pot plants up and down, he is moving closer to the stairs. Go on! Go on! Off you go. Neither Dennis nor I are really breathing, fearful that our very movement might pique his interest and bring him back to our end of Reception again. Then Patrick moves; the twat.

"Would any of you mind if I go and get myself a cup of coffee from downstairs," he says.

"No," says Dennis, his head lolling to one side.

"Oh, coffee," says Terrance, turning round and rubbing his hands together. "That sounds like a good idea."

"I'm afraid it is only staff coffee, for members of the staff," says Dennis quickly.

"Oh," says Terrance, sounding disappointed.

"It doesn't taste very nice," adds Dennis, in an attempt to sound polite. "If you do want some coffee," he says. "You'll have go back to your room and order it from Room Service and get it up there."

"Yes," I add somewhat unconsciously. "Go back to your room and have it there."

"Oh, I don't think I fancy it that much, after all," says Terrance, sitting back down on his sofa. "It might stop me from going back to sleep."

My telephone goes again and for some reason I think it must be the weeping woman from Number 306.

"Are you alright?" I ask immediately, without thinking.

"Not really," says a male voice.

"Oh, I'm sorry," I say. "I thought you were someone else."

"I can be someone else if you want."

"No don't worry. How can I help you?"

"Oh," he says. "You can really help me."

"Good."

"Oh. In fact you could really, really help me."

"Sir?"

"Mmm?" he replies. I think I can hear the sound of him wanking in the background. "Would you come up here and finish me off?" he asks.

"What?"

"Come up and blow me," he says.

"No, sir, I don't think I can."

"I'll pay you."

"No."

"Please."

"No, sir, I'm afraid that is not possible."

"Please," he says again.

"No."

"Is there anyone else in the hotel who would blow me for money?" he asks.

"No, sir," I say. "And I'm afraid I am going to have to put the phone down right now."

Perverts are always calling up in the middle of the night, asking for blow jobs or full sex. It is one of the hazards of doing the late shift that you have to deal with those sorts of calls. That is one of the reasons why the management doesn't particularly like putting women on the desk on their own (although they do), as they tend to get quite a lot of abuse. Drunken men calling up and demanding blow jobs from the front-of-house staff are not that unusual. The waiters and barmen get propositioned all the time. Some are offered money to make late-night visits to bedrooms and I have known a couple of guys who have actually gone and done it. But it is a very dangerous game to play. However, perhaps it is danger that makes it so appealing.

That's not to say that the female guests aren't equally as predatory. The coffee-throwing woman who went after me tonight is not a rarity. Waiters and bar staff are getting goosed and asked up to the rooms by women all the time. I did hear a story recently from a mate of mine who is working in New York about a businesswoman who asked for butler service for the weekend, and then spent the entire three days fucking her butler. I wonder if he charged her for extras?

But it's the calls from outside the hotel that can sometimes be very upsetting. We get all sorts calling up, and not only just old guests who want to be talked through a recipe or two. We did use to have a heavy breather who, I think, must have been watching the hotel, or perhaps lived near by, and walked past to check and see who was on Reception, because he would only call up when one of the girls was at the desk on her own. He'd say things like "I can see you" and describe what the girls were wearing before wanking himself off on the phone. We did get the police involved, but there is very little that they can do in that sort of situation.

We also get depressives and potential suicides calling up. It's dreadful, and often heart-breaking stuff. I suppose they call because they know that, whatever the time of day or night, someone will answer the telephone, and they just need to talk to somebody. We do have the phone number for Samaritans at hand, but sometimes they just want to chat.

Last week, I had some bloke on the phone who was threatening to kill himself and it was enough to give me nightmares. Which it did, actually, for at least a couple of nights afterwards. He was drunk and rambling and saying that he was going to take these pills. It's one of those things, you know: you want to help, but you don't know where to begin. I made him tell me about his girlfriend, who had walked out on him, taking his child. Eventually, I got him to give me his address and Dennis called up the police. I don't know what happened to the bloke, we don't tend to be kept in the loop. But Dennis assures me he wouldn't have topped himself: he says that if a man really wants to kill himself, he goes ahead and does it right away. He doesn't call anyone, or tell people that he is going to take pills. If he does that, then he has no intention of seeing the thing through. Women, on the other hand, according to Dennis, take pills when they know that someone will be coming home. They are often more attention-seeking than men. I'm not sure if he's right, but I do like to think that I managed to stop the bloke from killing himself. It makes me sleep better that way.

Talking of sleep, I can't believe Terrance is still sitting on the yellow sofa. He appears to be one of our more determined Dressing Gown Men.

"Have you ever thought about taking pills to help you sleep, Terrance?" I ask, for want of something to say to him.

"Funny you should ask that," says Terrance, leaning forward, opening his legs. I try and keep eye contact with the man, for fear of what might now be on display.

"Really?"

"Yes. I took a couple of them earlier, and they didn't seem to make a blind bit of difference."

"Oh," I say, nodding.

"Very interesting," says Dennis.

"Isn't it?" says Terrance. "But then again, I find they don't often work. I'm just one of those people who clearly doesn't need much sleep."

"Mmm," says Dennis.

"Margaret Thatcher used to survive on four hours a night, you know," shares Terrance.

"That would explain a lot," says Dennis.

"Ha, ha, ha," laughs Terrance.

While Terrance is laughing with unnecessary exuberance at Dennis's amazingly quick wit, a large white van pulls up outside the hotel. Dennis is up out of his chair and clicks his fingers at Patrick to follow suit. The morning newspapers have arrived, and the two of them go out to meet the deliveryman to help him in with the bundles. Dennis always seems to like this job: he stands for a good ten minutes outside with the bloke while Patrick struggles back and forth with the heavy piles of newspapers. This van does all the luxury hotels at once, and Dennis likes to be the first with the gossip, picking up any tidbits he can. He is laughing, joking, chatting, and blowing on his hands as he stands outside. Neither of the two men pay any attention to Patrick; they only turn around to acknowledge him after the job is over. Dennis pats the deliveryman on the back and comes back inside.

"Jesus Christ, it is cold enough to freeze brass monkeys out there," he says, still blowing on his hands. "Apparently they've had quite a party tonight at Claridge's. There are pissed posh people in black tie littered all over Mayfair searching for cabs. Jeff there," he points outside to where the newspaper van had pulled up. "He says that he thinks it was some film party or something; he swears he saw a couple of stars reeling their way up the street. Let's a get a few papers out, to see if it's in them," he walks towards the pile.

"You're not really supposed to read those before we hand them round to the guests," I say.

"Fuck it," says Dennis, bending down with a pair of scissors at the ready. "None of them will notice."

With the arrival of the newspapers detracting attention away from him, Terrance decides to call it a night.

"I can't believe it is almost morning," he says, looking at the newspapers. "I think I better just lie down, even if I don't actually manage to sleep."

"Yes, OK then," says Dennis.

"Good night," he says.

"Good night," I reply.

"Don't work too hard," he says with a small smile, before getting into the elevator.

"We won't," says Dennis, as the elevator door closes. "Thank God for that," he says, as Terrance finally disappears.

"Oh, I know," I say. "He'd never go."

"I don't know what you are complaining about," says Dennis. "You didn't have to listen to his whole bloody life story."

"I did a bit," I say.

"Fuck off, you did," says Dennis. "You ran off on any and every bloody errand that you could think of, so as not to have to talk to the dull bastard. Honestly," he says. "Next time I'm on nights with you and we get another Dressing Gown Bore, you are going to have to talk to him. He was driving me mad."

"He wasn't that bad," says Patrick, almost out of earshot.

"What?" says Dennis, his head turning swiftly in Patrick's direction.

"He wasn't that bad," he says again.

"Yes, he was, he was a boring bastard," says Dennis. "Anyway you, why aren't you polishing shoes?"

"Oh," says Patrick.

"Yes, 'oh,'" says Dennis, imitating him. "Shouldn't you be off around the hotel picking up shoes to polish by now? Or are you forgetting how to do your job?"

"No, sir," says Patrick.

"Yes, sir," says Dennis, indicating towards the stairs with his head. "And hurry up about it. People will be wanting those soon. Get to it. Now!"

Patrick rushes off up the stairs. Truth be known, he is actually rather late to be collecting shoes at this time. He should have been standing there, brushing away, for at least an hour. Fortunately for him, it is Saturday today, so there won't be that many pairs of shoes waiting to be done, and there won't be any demanding financial district boys who are desperate to get their shoes back for their 7:00 A.M. breakfast meeting. If it were a weekday morning, I have to say, Patrick would have been in some serious shit right now. I just hope there are no guests with early planes to catch.

It is looking distinctly lighter outside now, but I still have quite a way to go before I can even think about going home. I am so tired now that I'm actually finding it hard to concentrate, and there is a metallic taste in my mouth. The lights are too bright and I am beginning to feel really quite cold. I get some more Pro-Plus out of my pocket and try to swallow them without any water. Jesus, they taste bitter; I really hope they'll do the trick.

Dennis is going through the morning papers looking for the Claridge's party story, to see if there were indeed any celebrities at the soiree, or milling around afterwards on the streets of Mayfair. Patrick comes downstairs with his arms loaded with pairs of shoes in felt drawstring bags. He has seven pairs altogether. All of which, so he says, belong to Mr. Masterson. He lays them all out in his area near the luggage trolley and both Dennis and I go over to have a look.

"Well, they aren't designer," says Patrick, holding them up. "I never heard of Lobb, have you?"

"They're all handmade especially for him," says Dennis, picking up one of the shoes and examining it at close range. "This is some very expensive footwear, my son. Look and learn, Patrick, look and learn." He smiles. "And don't fuck it up."

"No, sir," says Patrick, sniffing the leather. "They smell great."

"Yeah, well," says Dennis. "There is no need to go that far, mate. Did you get the breakfast hangers while you were up there?"

"You never said," stammers Patrick, suddenly looking pink and sweaty. "Honestly, had you asked me . . ."

"I'll go," I say. "Dennis, mate, I could to do with the walk, I'm falling asleep here."

"All right. Next time," he says to Patrick, "try and do a couple of jobs at once, you'll find you might save yourself some time."

I set off around the hotel collecting breakfast hangers. It should normally be a Room Service job, but for some reason in this place, it falls to front-of-house. One of the things that always makes me laugh about breakfast hangers is that, when you stay at a place, you're always told that you have to leave the hangers out on the doors before 11:30 P.M. But we never come and collect them until around 4:30 A.M. We're far too busy with drunks and prostitutes to even think about collecting before then. Just so long as you get your hanger out before dawn, I guarantee you'll get your breakfast. At least that's true in this place.

It's the weekend, so there will be many more breakfast slips than during the week. During the week, most of the business guys are up and out for meetings before 7:00 A.M. so they rarely manage to eat before they go. But come Saturday, there is nothing a weekender likes more than a big fat fry-up, or some scrambled eggs and champagne.

It is always a bit eerie, walking along these corridors at this time of night. It's dark and quiet, and the only thing that stops you from thinking that the place is empty is the constant snoring accompaniment that guides you along each floor. You wouldn't believe the different snoring pitches there are—high lady snores, the deeper baritone male, and what can only be described as some sort of low-growling marsh dweller, who manages to vibrate the paintings in the corridor as well as the bedroom doors.

On my way back down the stairs, my hands full of breakfast hangers, I can hear some scratching along the corridor on the fourth floor. I stand still, my ears straining to hear it above the snores. My toes curl in my shoes; I stare into the darkness wondering what vile piece of vermin has been missed by the man from Rentokil. My catering trousers are really itching, but I have no time for that, as I sidle my way along to the end of the corridor.

The Honor Bar lights are on. From the loud amount of rattling going on, the rat sounds like it must be enormous. As I turn the corner, I hear the noise of the fridge door opening and I am greeted with the image of a tramp who is standing, backside facing me, with his head in the minibar, rootling around for alcohol.

"Oi!" I shout, striding into the bar all authoritative and in-charge. "What the hell are you doing?" The tramp leaps out of his skin and whacks his head on the fridge door. Judging by the collection of empties that are lined up on the side, he looks like he's been in here for some time, knocking back the booze.

"Oh shit," he slurs, clearly trying to focus on me. He is definitely the worse for wear and alcohol. "I was just . . ." He stops. He knows that he has been caught with his hands in the fridge, so there is little use in trying to argue his way out of this situation. He holds his hands in tatty finger-less gloves up in the air, like we are in some sort of shoot-out. "I'll come quietly," he says. "Only please don't call the police."

"Come on," I say, grabbing the back of his coat. There is a rattle of glass. "What have you got in your pockets?"

"Oh, nothing," he says.

"Empty them."

"You can't make me do that," he protests.

"Well, it's either me or the police," I say.

"OK then," he says, shoving his hands into his pockets and pulling out a whole load of Bombay Sapphire miniatures. He has loads of them—six in his right pocket and a whole fistful in his left. He places them all on the side.

"Anything else?" I say.

"Nothing."

"How about your inside pockets?"

"Well . . ."

"Come on," I say. "Do you really want me to call the police? Because I am very happy to do that."

"No," he says, swaying slightly, as he pulls open his coat to reveal a small clutch of Penhaligon's bottles.

"Shampoo?" I ask. "What do you want shampoo for?"

"I don't know." He shrugs. "The cupboard door was open, so I helped myself."

"Oh," I say, as he puts all the small plastic bottles and three small soaps back on the side. "What is it with the Bombay Sapphire?"

"I like it," he says. "It's my favorite drink."

"Right," I say. "Can I just say you look a bit familiar?"

"Right." He nods, looking at the floor.

"You've been here before."

"A couple of times," he says.

"This week," I add.

"Possibly."

"Have you taken Bombay Sapphire with you every time you have been here?"

"Might have done," he says sounding like a teenager.

"Well, I think you have."

"Think what you want."

"I will."

"You can't fucking prove anything."

"I can," I say. "I found you in here with your hands in the fridge and your pockets full of booze. What more proof do I need?"

"That doesn't prove anything," he says.

"It does," I say. Then I stop myself. What the hell am I doing? Why am I bothering to try to reason with a tramp at 4:45 A.M. in the Honor Bar? This does have to be one of the more surreal aspects of the job. "Right, come on," I say.

"Come on where?"

"Out."

"Oh, come on," he moans.

"No, out," I say. "You can't stay here. Come on."

He doesn't bother to kick up a fuss. He turns around and pockets two small bottles of Bombay Sapphire gin before he ac-

companies me off towards the elevator. I decide not to say anything; Tony will be so pleased to have his Sapphire thief stopped,
he won't mind a couple more miniatures missing. We travel
down in silence in the elevator. It grows progressively less fra-
grant, the longer we stand in this confined space together. When
the doors finally open on the ground floor, I am relieved to get
into some fresh air. After that small trip together, part of me
wishes I had given him the shampoo as well, before sending him
on his way.

"Shit," says Dennis, as we come into Reception. "It's not you
again, is it, Spike?" Dennis rolls his eyes. "How many more
bloody times do we have to throw you out of here before you
know that you are not allowed in here? Mmmm? How many?"
Dennis seems to have this amazing ability to make a tramp appear sheepish. Spike shuffles along looking at the floor. "Don't
worry, mate." Dennis says to me. "I'll take Spike from here."
Dennis walks up to Spike and puts his arm around his shoulder
and escorts him to the door. "Come along now, Spike," he says.
"Next time, I'll call the police. Honestly, mate, I will, and I'm
not kidding."

I watch as Dennis takes Spike outside. He is not rude or un-
pleasant to him, in fact, as the two of them talk outside on the
street, I see Dennis reach into his pocket and pull out a note,
handing it over. He then slaps Spike on his back, sending him on
his way.

"Did you just give Spike some money?" I ask, as Dennis
comes back in to sit down at the desk.

"What? Me?" he says, acting all shocked. "What do you take
me for?"

"Oh." I know he is lying.

Dennis and I sit in silence. All I can hear is a brushing sound
coming from Patrick's corner: he is still hard at work polishing
shoes. My stomach starts to rumble; I really fancy having some-

thing to eat. The breakfast chefs should be here in minutes, I think, as I lean on my desk; I could really murder a bacon sandwich. I could go down and pester the blokes doing the all-night room service, making chicken salads, club sandwiches, and burgers, but quite frankly, I always think that none of those guys can really cook; half of them would burn water.

Just as I have completed the list of people whom I would actually kill for a bacon sandwich, the breakfast chefs come in the door.

The two of them arrive together. They both look thin and cold as they walk into Reception.

"Morning," says one of them.

"Is it?" says Dennis.

"As far as I'm concerned, it is," says the other.

"How long before you've got some bacon on the go?" asks Dennis, reading my mind.

"Yes," I say. "How long?"

"Five or ten," says the taller of the two.

"Fantastic," says Dennis, rubbing his hands. "We'll be down in a second."

It's not really these guys' jobs to cook breakfast for us. But they do it all the same. They are supposed to get everything ready for the big breakfast push at about 8:00 A.M. They are supposed to parcook all the sausages and bacon so that all they have to do is reheat the ingredients to get the breakfasts out on time.

My mouth is filling with saliva: I'll eat my hand soon, if I'm not careful.

The telephone goes.

"Hello, Reception."

"Why are we here?" comes this weird female voice.

"I'm sorry," I say.

"Why are we here? Who are we?" she says.

"I'm sorry, I have no idea," I say, and hang up.

"Who was that?" asks Dennis.

"It's that woman who has been staying here for a couple of days locked in her room," I say, thinking about bacon. "She was asking all sorts of weird things."

"Oh," says Dennis.

The phone goes again.

"Hello."

"You hung up on me," she says.

"Um, sorry."

"No one hangs up on me," she says. "No one. I'm coming down." She hangs up.

"Oh shit," I say to Dennis. "The weird woman is on her way down."

Dennis and I sit and watch the elevator, waiting for the mad-woman to come down. I suppose it is a bit unfair of me to call her mad, but she has been in the hotel for three days now and no one, apart from the guys doing room service, has seen her.

We do get guests who book in occasionally for a bit of splen-did isolation, but they are usually men, and they are usually on some drug binge or other. Rich junkies, who want to take their heroin in peace, or cokeheads who have a three-day party with fellow cocaine-takers and then leave, looking like they've been exhumed. I remember a group of new Russian boys who came here and booked themselves into three suites. They had about three unfeasibly pretty dolly birds with them, and bags of co-caine. They closed the bedroom curtains and did not leave the hotel all weekend. They ordered something like thirty bottles of Cristal Champagne and almost nothing to eat. When they left on the Sunday, I contemplated calling an ambulance, they looked so ill.

Dennis and I still have our eyes on the elevator, as it counts down the floors. The bell rings, it arrives on the ground floor and the doors open. We both brace ourselves. Nothing. The woman is nowhere to be seen. Dennis sits back in his seat, and I put another foul-tasting mint in my mouth.

"She's changed her mind," I suggest, watching the elevator doors close.

"Looks like it," says Dennis.

"That's a relief," I say.

"Mmm."

"Do you think the bacon is ready yet?" I ask. "My stomach is so hungry it is eating itself."

"Um," says Dennis, looking at his watch. "Give it a couple of minutes."

I start scratching again. The sooner I get home, the sooner I can get out of these trousers. I wonder if the man who knocked himself out on the urinal is OK. Perhaps one of us should ring the hospital and find out.

"Do you think the Urinal Man is OK?" I ask Dennis.

"What? Yeah, I'm sure. We would have heard something, otherwise."

"Yeah. You're right . . . How are you doing with your shoes there, Patrick?" I ask, leaning my head forward over the desk.

"Only one more left." He waves a shiny shoe in my direction. "Then that's it."

"You better show them to me before you take them up," says Dennis.

"Are you suggesting that I don't know how to shine shoes?" asks Patrick, sounding a touch offended.

"No. It's just that we have standards."

"Yeah, right." Patrick laughs.

Their conversation is interrupted by the sound of a loud off-key singing on the stairs. "Da da da, da da da, New York! New York!" We turn and look up the stairs as the madwoman comes down, one step at a time, high-kicking like a showgirl. She is wearing her complimentary toweling robe, but it hangs open at the front and underneath she is stark naked. "Da da da, da da da," she sings. "Da da da, da da da," she kicks. "Da da da, da da, New York! New York!" Both Dennis and I are so shocked, we can't move. Patrick carries on brushing his shoe, his face trained on the woman, his mouth wide open. The woman doesn't look like she can actually see anyone or, indeed, where she is going. She stares in front of her, her head held high, her eyes are shining in a demonic fashion. She looks like she is lost in the world of show. Her face is sheet-white, the bags under her eyes are dark red, and her very-bleached blond hair stands on end. It would actually be funny, if it weren't so disturbing.

She continues on down the stairs, still singing "New York, New York" and walks, kicking her legs towards me. She has me locked in her sights, like I am the only member of her very private audience. She swings her naked hips and takes off an imaginary glove, like a stripper in a nightclub. Flinging it around her head, she throws it at me. She seems disappointed that I don't rush to catch it. "New York, New York!" she sings, and then, in one swift action, takes her dressing gown off altogether. She stands totally naked in front of me and then says, "There, that got your attention, didn't it?"

The elevator bell goes, and a man comes, all suited, out of the elevator. He doesn't notice the woman at first; he is too busy fiddling with his tie. When he does, he stops dead in his tracks and stares. She ignores him or doesn't notice him, either way, she doesn't even flinch.

"Morning, sir," I say, as he stands there.

"Morning," he says, rather quietly.

"Checking out?"

"Um, yes," he says. "Room 214."

"214," I repeat, trying to sound normal. "Right away."

The woman doesn't seem at all perturbed at the increase in the size of her audience. She carries on, swaying from side to side, staring at me and singing "New York, New York" softly under her breath. Her dressing gown is gathered around her feet like a puddle of water.

"How will you be paying, sir?" I ask.

"What?" he says, staring at the naked dancing woman. "Oh, right," he says, gathering his thoughts. "Visa."

"Visa," I repeat.

"Yes," he says, rattling around the inside top pocket of his suit.

"Anything from the minibar, sir?"

"Um, yes. A bottle of red wine."

"Just the one?"

"Yes."

"No water or nuts or anything?"

"No."

"Right, sir, that's £385.70."

"Good." He hands over the card.

"Would you like to check the bill?"

"No," he says slowly. "I have a plane to catch."

"Right, of course."

I go into the back office and run his card through the machine. I can feel the madwoman's stare boring into my back. I can still hear her muttered rendition of "New York, New York" behind me.

"Good stay, sir?" I hear Dennis trying to make pleasant conversation.

"Yes, thank you."

"First time?" Dennis carries on valiantly.

"What? No," says the man. "Third."

"Third," says Dennis, sounding impressed. "I think I'd call you, sir, a regular."

"Yes," says the man, looking so relieved as I come out of the office bearing his credit card slip to sign. He scribbles his signature and picks up his bag and makes a dash for the door.

"Do you want your receipt, sir?" I ask.

"No," he calls back. "You keep it."

"Can I get you a cab?"

"No, thank you," he says, as he hurls himself through the revolving doors.

"OK," I say in a breezy voice. "Dennis," I say, maintaining the same tone of voice. "I think you'd better call the police or an ambulance or something."

"Do you know?" says Dennis, sounding equally as jolly. "I might just try that 999 service."

"You do that." I smile. "Right away."

I walk slowly around the desk, keeping eye contact with the naked dancing woman through the tropical flower display. I keep an inane smile on my face, as I nod along to her tuneless singing. I approach her with caution and very slowly I bend down to pick up her dressing gown. She points at me like some provocative show girl. I slowly stand up and put the dressing gown around her shoulders in an attempt to claw back some of her dignity. But she starts to scream at the top of her voice. She turns around and tries to pull the toweling off her back.

"GET IT OFF ME! GET IT OFF ME! GET IT OFF ME!" she yells. Her voice is deep and demonic, she sounds possessed.

Dennis looks shocked, as he talks on the telephone. "D'you hear that?" he says. "I have a feeling this is serious. Some sort of drug-induced psychosis."

I back off, holding my hands in the air. This woman is really quite scary. I actually don't want to have anything to do with her. If she wants to sing show tunes while stark naked in Reception, then who am I to interfere?

"Well, that's good," says Dennis, in a singsong voice. "They'll be around in a couple of minutes."

"Just a couple?" I say.

"Oh yes," he says back.

"In the meantime?"

"In the meantime," he says, "let's enjoy the show."

"OK," I say, my voice sounding high and tight.

The madwoman is bored with staring at me, and seems to be more interested in the chandelier above her head. She starts to dance in a circle, staring skywards, snaking her arms around her swaying body. I don't what she is singing any more: it sounds like a song of her own composition. Dennis and I look at each other across the room; he shrugs and does one of those circular, "crazy" gestures at his temple. I am just relieved that she has found another audience.

The police are as good as their word: they arrive within a few minutes. They approach the naked woman quite carefully: they move forward tentatively. Not that she is noticing a thing; she keeps staring up at the ceiling, doing her Queen of Sheba dance.

"Excuse me, hello, excuse me," says the policewoman. "How long has she been like this?" she asks me.

"About ten minutes," I say. "But she has been in her room on her own for three days now."

"Three days?" asks the policewoman.

"Yes."

The policewoman picks up the dressing gown and makes to put it on the woman's back.

"I wouldn't do that, if I were you," I say. Too late. The policewoman puts the dressing gown on and all hell breaks loose: the madwoman screams and screams. We really can't have her here any more; she is going to start waking up the other guests. She starts to roll around on the floor patting her arms and back, like the dressing gown has set fire to her skin.

"I think we should take her," says the policewoman. "Get her to hospital to see what drugs she has been taking."

"That would be good," says Dennis. "As we do have a hotel to run."

"Do you know what her name is?" asks the policewoman.

"Um," I say. "I could find out." I look on the register and come up with Parker. "Miss Parker."

"OK, Miss Parker," says the policewoman. "Me and my colleague here are going to help you."

Miss Parker doesn't even appear to recognize her own name. She carries on, spinning around naked in the middle of Reception. Then through the front door comes a policeman carrying what looks like a white straitjacket—Jesus, they look frightening. I can't look: all I can do is listen to her scream as she is wrestled to the ground. I hear her flail around on the floor, while three people pin her down and strap her into the jacket. I know there is no other way of getting her out of here and getting her help, but that doesn't make it any more palatable. By the time I feel able to turn around, they have her all strapped in and they are dragging her out towards the van. She is still shouting and screaming and swearing at the top her voice. Her slim white legs are still trying to run away, but she is going nowhere.

As she goes out through the revolving doors, another guest is on his way in, straight off a plane from somewhere. His face looks a picture of shock and horror.

"My God," he says, as he dumps his bags at Reception. "What happened to her?"

"She refused to pay the bill," declares Dennis from the other side of the room. "We do that to all our guests."

"Oh," says the guest, looking confused.

"Don't worry." I smile reassuringly. "He is only joking. What is your name please, sir?"

I check in a rather confused and disturbed Mr. Armstrong. You can tell he is asking himself if he really wants to stay here for a whole week. Also, when I tell him that he'll have to wait for his room, as it has yet to be made up, he looks like he is about to walk straight back out of the hotel. But then I remind him he should have made a prereg booking if he expected to be allowed to check in this early; he shuts up, and walks rather slowly into the dining room, to wait until they start serving breakfast. This is normally 7:00 A.M. on the weekend, but I did say that I'd go downstairs into the kitchen to see if they would make an exception.

Downstairs, the kitchen is buzzing with a bit more life. The stoves are on, there is a smash and rattle of activity, the chatter of conversation and all the while, the smell of frying bacon competes with that of chlorine. The two chefs seem to have a lot more than bacon and sausages on the go: they've already made a pile of toast and a vat of scrambled eggs by the time I get in there.

Just as I start to negotiate a full English breakfast for the tired Mr. Armstrong in the hotel dining room, the head chef turns up. He's very early: there must be a wedding or something on today. I've worked with him before; his name is Matthew, and he is a temperamental old bastard. I start to explain the situation, and he brushes me away with a wave of his hand, pretending that he can't hear above the noise of the kitchen.

"Please," I find myself saying. "It would really make our life so much easier."

"I'm not here to make your life easier," he declares. "Rules are rules and they are not allowed to be broken. The guests don't get their breakfasts until 7:00 A.M. He'll just have to wait."

I'm so tired and pissed off by him that I march out of the kitchen. I turn around and give him the finger; he pretends not to notice, but I know he does. Even then, it doesn't make me feel any better. I walk into the staff dining room, thinking I might make Dennis and myself each a bacon sandwich. There are about seven Bangladeshi cleaners in there when I come in, they are all chatting away to each other, eating some sort of curry dish that the kitchen makes especially, or, should I say, reheats, especially for them. They all ignore me as I go up to the hot plate and look through the stainless steel trays. There are a few slices of bacon in a bowl; they are still bright pink and the fat is barely cooked—they must have been frying for about a minute at most. There is some white bread in a pile that was toasted a while back: it is now stretchy and springy like a trampoline. I butter the toast and make two sandwiches, making sure that I cover Dennis's in brown sauce. (I've made enough sandwiches for him not to make the mistake of leaving stuff off ever again.) Helping myself to a couple of paper plates, I turn around to leave the dining room. On my way out, I bump into the Iraqi doctor whom I'd spoken to earlier, I smile. He looks the other way, and neither of us speaks to the other.

Back upstairs, and Dennis is on his desk phone. He is on hold for one of the airlines. It's his job at about this time in the morning to ring and check to see if any flights are delayed, or if any have come in early, so we can find out who to expect for early check-in. It's not so vital on a Saturday morning, but it is in the middle of the week, when we have rooms to vacate, and others to clean and businessmen on their way from Heathrow. These vital minutes, or half hours, can make all the difference between keeping a New Yorker waiting in Reception, or getting him straight up into his room.

Dennis gets off the phone. "There's snow in Washington," he says. "And some fog in Paris, but apart from that, all the flights appear to be on time."

"Right," I say. What Dennis is forgetting is that I don't really care. I've one hour left and I'm just desperate to get through it with the minimum amount of fuss and effort. I am even rather hoping that, after my bacon sandwich, I might have a quick forty winks on the desk.

"Those bacon?" asks Dennis, as he walks towards the desk.

"Yup. And brown sauce, just how you like it."

"You'd make someone a great wife one day," says Dennis, as he follows me into the back office to eat his breakfast. It wouldn't be a good look for either of us to be caught eating in Reception, and that is why they gave us the back room; we're always popping in and out of there to eat a sandwich or a bag of potato chips. It also goes some way to explaining why the place smells so much. Dennis eats his sandwich in about three mouthfuls: he's a man who is clearly too busy to chew. I take a bit more time, savoring every single distinctly inorganic mouthful. But when I'm only halfway through, someone rings the Reception bell. I come through the door to be confronted by the woman who threw a pot of coffee at the door after I wouldn't have sex with her. She is standing there with her husband.

"Good morning," I say.

"Good morning," she says, looking down into her handbag like nothing ever happened. She does at least have the decency to blush.

I check out the coffee-hurler and her husband with the minimum of fuss. The weird thing is, looking at her in the pale purple light of dawn, she is a lot more attractive than the night-vision version of herself, and I kind of wish I had slept with her. She has a pretty turned-up nose, large lips that curl up at the corners, lots of thick blond hair and she does sheepish very well indeed. I notice, as I hand back her credit card, that her name is Ciara. That's always been one of my favorite names. Next time, I think, as I watch her walk away. Jesus, I must be tired, if I am even thinking this way.

Dennis is back on his cell phone again, telling another relative of his the story about the naked woman singing in Reception. He's telling it like it is a joke; it sounds much better in the telling than it did in the witnessing. I can hear the person on the other end of the telephone hooting with laughter. I do like Dennis—nothing ever really seems to touch him.

A couple of the kitchen staff and a few of the chambermaids are already coming into the hotel for early breakfasts. Some of them come from miles away, they leave home early so that public transportation doesn't make them late and then they make the most of their spare time by having a spot of breakfast.

Mr. Armstrong comes out into Reception. The man looks tired, hungry, and a little pissed off. I have to admit that, in my quest for my own bacon sandwich, I had rather forgotten that he was sitting there, waiting to be served.

"Any idea when I might get some food?" he asks.

"Any minute now." I smile.

"Right," he says, not sounding at all convinced.

"There isn't even anyone serving in the dining room," he says. "I haven't spotted a waiter in the half hour that I have been sitting in there. Just a cup of coffee, something," he says, sounding more desperate than pissed off.

"I'd go back and sit in the dining room, sir," I say. "I'll send someone in to take your order and bring you a pot of coffee."

"Please," he says. "And hurry up about it."

"Right away, sir," I say, as breezily as twenty-four hours standing perpendicular will let me.

I call down to Room Service in the kitchen. It takes an age for someone to answer the phone. I ask them to bring a pot of coffee into the dining room and to get one of the breakfast waiters out of the staff canteen, and into the guests' dining room to take Mr. Armstrong's order. I have to make this request three times: either the bloke on the other end doesn't understand English, or he is being deliberately obstreperous. I've just about had enough of this job, this night, this life. I have less than an hour to go, and I swear to God I am counting down the minutes; I keep looking at the clock on the switchboard. I have been doing it so much in the past ten minutes or so that I am going to have to ration my-self, otherwise the clock won't appear to be moving at all.

Dennis is still chatting away on his cell. I think, next time I do a shift with him, I'm going to ask him to switch it off. Patrick suddenly stops his polishing and announces that he has finished doing his shoes, and walks over to Dennis to show him. I thought he'd done them all hours ago, but apparently not. From over here, Dennis looks impressed. He holds each shoe up to the light, checking to see if the soles and the heels are clean. He pats Patrick on the back, gives him the thumbs-up, and sends him on his way to Mr. Masterson's suite. Patrick looks pleased with himself as he stands by the elevator: his pale skin has a bit of color to it. It is amazing what praise does to a lad's complexion.

My phone goes.

"Reception," I say.

It's one of the Room Service boys and he is outside old Mrs. Robertson's room, bringing her morning tea, except she is not answering the door. He's been knocking on her door for the past couple of minutes and he can't hear anything. I explain that it's not odd that he can't hear anything, because neither can she. But I do also feel that it is a little strange. Mrs. Robertson has had her cup of tea delivered to her room at 6:15 A.M. every day since she moved in here two and half years ago—it is one of the hotel routines; it sort of marks the beginning of the day—Mrs. Robert-son gets her tea, and we all change shifts. So it is odd that she is not answering. I offer to phone up, and see if I can wake her. I dial the number; the phone rings out, and I wait for a long while before hanging up. Her television can't be on, so she must be able to hear it. I have an odd sensation in my stomach, and I don't like the way I am feeling.

I tell Dennis that I am off upstairs to check on something and he seems to register. All the way up in the elevator, I have but-terflies in my stomach, and I am beginning to feel sick. I arrive on the top floor, and walk to the end of the corridor, where I find the young lad with Mrs. Robertson's morning tea now getting cold, as he stands anxiously outside her door.

"Have you tried knocking again?" I ask.

"Many times," he says, his face looking white and strained. "I have brought her morning tea almost every day for the past year," he says. "And she always answers the door." We both look at each other. I glimpse a terrified and yet resigned look in his eyes: we both know what we will find once I open the door.

"Mrs. Robertson," I shout hopefully, hammering on the door again. He joins in, his fists banging away, sounding even more desperate than mine. "I think I should open the door," I suggest, reaching in my pocket for my pass card. The young man recoils, he takes two steps back and shakes his head. His eyes start to shine, I can see he is about to cry. "I'll go in first," I say. "You don't have to come in." He doesn't say anything; he stands with his back to the corridor wall, firmly holding on to his tray.

I open the door to her bedroom and walk in. The curtains are closed, and it is still dark inside. The air is very still indeed: the bedroom smells of mothballs, lavender, and the sweet, high aroma of talc, but it feels like there is no oxygen at all. I walk over to the other side of the room and draw the curtains. I also open the window. I read somewhere that when someone dies you should always do that—it releases the spirit or something. I turn around towards the bed, and see Mrs. Robertson lying there. She is flat on her back, the bedding pulled up tight around her neck, her thin hands are still holding onto the sheets. The woman is definitely dead, I can tell from here, I don't need to put a mirror in front of her face to check to see if she is still breathing. I walk over to take a closer look. Her eyes are firmly shut, her mouth is the slightest bit open, but her face looks hollow; she looks tiny, all skin and bone. She wasn't exactly enormous when alive, but in death, she looks half the size. They say the soul weighs twenty-one grams, well, hers must have been a hell of a lot heavier than that.

I hear the Room Service boy come in behind me. He walks slowly towards the bed and squeaks when he sees the body. He stands with his hands over his mouth, he starts to shake and a silent tear runs down his cheek. It must be the first time he has seen a dead body. This is my third.

You'd be amazed how many people die in hotels: I'm sure they must be second only to hospitals for corpses. Hotel deaths fall into two separate categories: there are some who have every intention of dying there when they check in, and there are others, of course, who do it by accident. Take Mrs. Robertson, for example; both she and the staff always knew that she would die here. After her husband passed on, she chose this hotel as the place where she wanted to end her days. There are other guests who do the same: hotels are a popular choice for people who want to commit suicide. You can see why—you book yourself into a room, and no one will disturb you for days at a time, unless you want them to. It sounds odd, but I sometimes think committing suicide in a hotel is a way of sparing the family: the discovery of the body, the clean-up, and the aftermath are all dealt with by strangers; the family doesn't have to be involved at all.

Then, of course, there are the people who die by accident: drug overdoses, heart attacks, sexual misadventure, choking on their vomit, or even falling over when drunk, like the man in the urinals earlier on tonight. I have only come across one heart attack victim so far. He'd taken too much cocaine while sleeping with a prostitute and died on the job. Half the guys working in the hotel couldn't think of a better way to go. However, I think if they'd seen the body, they might have changed their minds. It was not a pretty sight.

Mrs. Robertson is my second death by natural causes. The other was an old man in a hotel I worked in before. It was a bit of a nightmare, actually: he wasn't the nicest of blokes, and, if I am being honest, the hotel didn't notice for a couple of days. He wasn't a long-termer: he'd booked in for a short stay, and we'd all rather taken a bit of a dislike to him. When he didn't answer his door for breakfast, it was just left outside his door, as was breakfast again the next day. It was only in the afternoon of the second day that someone thought it a little odd that no one had had sight nor sound of the bloke, and, to be honest, the chambermaids wanted to get in to clean the room. I was dispatched to try and raise him and then eventually open his door. He was stiff as a board when I got in there and had obviously been dead for quite a while. We called the police and an ambulance crew, and informed all the relevant people. But when the ambulance crew turned up to take him away, there was a bit of a problem. We had a wedding blocking the whole of Reception and the ambulance couldn't get anywhere near the front of the hotel, so we had to bring him down the back stairs and out through the kitchens. I know you shouldn't laugh at the dead, but for some reason, it was very funny. We wrapped him up in a blanket and hauled him down the stairs. One of my old mates dropped him as we came through the kitchen, and we all almost cried with laughter. God knows what Health and Safety would have said.

Mrs. Robertson is obviously a little different: I really liked the old dear; she was sweet and elegant and lovely to everyone, tipping ten pence for every cup of tea she had. The Room Service bloke standing next to me, with his nose running, obviously agrees. I call down to Reception to tell Dennis the sad news. And for once, he doesn't have very much to say. He gets all monosyllabic on me, and tells me to cover the body, come back downstairs, and let him call the emergency services.

I walk back over to Mrs. Robertson's bed and pull on the sheets. The Room Service bloke starts crossing himself and muttering prayers in some foreign language, while I cover Mrs. Robertson's face. We both then leave the room, closing the door behind us. He bends down to pick up her tray of cold tea and we travel down in the elevator in silence.

Dennis seems to have gotten everything organized by the time we get there. He looks at me with a serious face as I walk back into Reception.

"Alright, mate?" he asks.

"Yeah." I nod. "It's not my first."

"Oh right," he says. "That's OK, then."

"Yeah. But it is the only one I really knew and liked, though."

"Yeah. She was a nice old bird."

I don't say anything. Instead, I walk into the back room to be on my own for a second, to try and get the image of her hollow face out of my head. I stand with my nose pressed against the window, clouding up the glass.

Through the fog, I can see the night staff leaving below. The cleaners are all changed out of their overalls and suddenly look like individuals. They are leaving in groups of two or three at a time, chatting away; they look animated and alive, unlike the sad ciphers whom I see every night scrubbing the floors. There is also a steady stream of chambermaids and kitchen staff all turning up for work; their heads are down and their collars are up against the wind. They go straight into the staff dining room for their free breakfasts.

The telephone in the office suddenly rings. I jump a bit and I answer it. It is some music PR person in a panic on her cell phone at Heathrow. She has got some band arriving in from America and wants to know if we can put them and their entourage up at the hotel. She mumbles something about the lead singer not wanting to go to the hotel the record company has booked. I tell her that unfortunately the hotel is full and we can't help her.

I'm not lying, but I might well have said the same thing, even if we had room: hotels are not big fans of entourages. Financially, we like them, as we always overcharge for the rooms; if you want eight rooms all on one floor, we tend to sting you for it, but only because we have to compensate ourselves for the trouble. I remember a heavyweight boxing champion hanging someone out of the window by his feet at the Grosvenor House Hotel. The hotel security couldn't do anything about it, because the boxer had come with his own musclemen. It's a scene that we can do without. Having said that, The Lanesborough was jumping with joy when Michael Jackson booked the whole of one floor. And then, of course, they charged him again when it came to the extras.

I come back out into Reception and Dennis tells me that the police and the ambulance crew have gone upstairs. Not that any foul play is expected, but they do have to go and make sure.

Someone calls down and asks me to prepare his bill, as he is leaving. I start the printout and notice he is yet another man who has been hitting the porn lines; he's spent £387.30. I sigh: I really hope that Liz gets here soon, before he comes down and starts arguing about the bill; I'm not in the mood for it. In fact, I am absolutely exhausted, I can't believe that I have made it to the end of my shift. I look at the Reception clock. I only have five minutes left. Dennis still has another hour to go, but he is already tidying up his papers and getting ready for the off.

Finally, I see Liz walking through the rain, coming towards the hotel; her body and umbrella are bent against the wind. My shoulders collapse slightly with the release of tension on seeing her; adrenaline pours out of my body so fast I feel like a rag doll. I feel weak and sick and I can barely see in front of me.

"Oh dear," says Liz, as she wafts back into Reception her blond hair blown, her face made up, her body well slept in and her skin smelling strongly of perfume. "You look terrible."

"Do I?" I reply, thinking, you don't look that goddamn super yourself.

"Tricky night?" she asks sarcastically.

"Not really." I smile, picking up my thin overcoat. "Nothing I couldn't handle. In fact, I might go so far as to say that it was really quite banal."

"Oh, right," she says, putting her coat in the back room and shaking out her umbrella, a tight smile on her lip-lined mouth. "Anything I should know about?"

"Nothing, really," I say nonchalantly. "I think some men will be appearing in a minute bringing a dead body down the front stairs."

"Yeah, right," she says, picking up her ballpoint pen and clicking it efficiently. "Good night."

"Night," I say, buttoning up my coat as I walk towards the door.

I'm really only putting one foot in front of the other in the hope that I will actually make it home. Come Monday morning, I'll be back at my desk to do the whole thing all over again.